THOMAS THE
TEMP JOB KING

THOMAS THE TEMP JOB KING

A Collection of My Most Interesting And Sometimes Comical Temporary Job Stories

Thomas Wayne Ratel

ISBN: 1506131913
ISBN 13: 9781506131917

Acknowledgments

To Bambi for her endless support and encouragement not only for the book but also for the actual temp jobs that she watched me head out to over the years.

Also, to my mom and the rest of my family and friends, many of whom enjoyed my temping stories at one time or another and suggested that I put it into print.

I am grateful to the office staff at my agency who were particularly supportive over the years, including, but not limited to Amy, Crystal, Janice, Sarah and Farah.

Thank you to Jade and all the other CreateSpace employees that helped me put this book together.

Finally, to past, current, and future temps who have or will have some stories of their own to share as well as the companies, small and large, along with the employees, kind or mean, who provided me with these stories in the first place.

Please feel free to read my temp blog or share stories of your own temp job adventures at thomasthetempjobking@squarespace.com

I'm also for hire so please feel free to inquire.

What Started It All

Between July 21, 1998, and March 17, 1999, I quit my longtime permanent job and began my Boston-area temporary-job saga. I traveled, caught up on some books, and just basically enjoyed my freedom. I was then ready to try something different. Years before, either in conversation or in print, I remembered hearing about the temp agency that I work for. I decided to call them up to see what they had to say. It happened to be St. Patrick's Day when they asked me to come in and fill out paperwork. I did go in and filled out lots of it without any idea what type of job(s) I was looking for, or what field. I was just about to leave the office after finishing my conversations with various office staffers, one of whom mentioned that 97 percent of the jobs were office related. Even though I didn't know what to expect going in, that news somehow deflated me. I had worked for years in an office environment, and I wasn't in any rush to do it again. I sort of wrote them off as I was leaving. But it was one young woman, Amy, who altered my life permanently coincidentally. She reached out to me with a positive attitude, assuring me there were plenty of other types of jobs besides office jobs. We sat down and talked of these other opportunities. Two days later I had my first taste of the sweetness of variety! I haven't looked back since.

Incredible Effort but No Reward Necessary

My goal since day one has been to give my utmost 100 percent effort for any job that comes along. I try to be the most conscientious worker in the world. I put forward all of my tireless energy, creative ideas, positive attitude, offbeat sense of humor, superhuman effort, and all that goes along with it. For these reasons, many times the companies at which I am placed try to hire me immediately. Although I'm flattered and humbled when I get offers, I always decline. More often than not, the potential employers get upset and sometimes even very angry. The stakes will sometimes go up, and they'll offer me more money, benefits, and so on. But my answer is still the same. Sometimes they feel offended and ask me what's wrong with them or their company. Mostly they are just absolutely puzzled as to why in the world I would pass up a great opportunity. I recall group meetings where I was stuck in a room with several managers scrutinizing and questioning me. It seems ridiculous that I'm sometimes in the hot seat for really no reason at all. When, in the end, I tell them that I'm happy with my agency and with what I'm doing, one of three things will happen: the company will eventually hire someone else permanently; they'll keep me as long as they are allowed to keep a temp; or they'll get rid of me right away since they are upset, which is extremely rare. Most often, they'll keep me as long as they can possibly hold a temp. When I began this adventure, I never realized that temp jobs are sometimes done in lieu of job interviews. Many companies would rather review a prospective employee rather than risk hiring a bum. It's also a two-way street. Workers will sometimes scope out a workplace as a temp. I'm by no means the smartest person around, but I do go all out when it comes to bringing passion to work.

Temping Is the Spice of My Life

Over the better part of two decades, I've done upward of a thousand combined temporary jobs, focus groups, medical or other research studies, mystery shops, blood donations, volunteer opportunities, and so forth. Never could I have imagined the richness added to my life or the crazy situations I'd find myself in, given my different experiences and encounters with various people. I'm certainly glad I took a leap of faith all those years ago. When asked what I do for a living, sometimes I say, "Oh, nothing," while other times I would *like* to say, "Ah, everything!" Of course, most were one-day gigs. Others, though, stretched for several years. Don't get me wrong. I've done plenty of mundane jobs, which is fine, since everything's temporary. I've been both overqualified and underqualified. I've worked with and for people ranging from janitors to CEOs and everything in between. I've worked for individuals, tiny companies and huge Fortune 500 companies. I've been my own boss and, in turn, have managed as many as fifty people at a time. I never refuse a job unless I physically can't make it for whatever reason. I'm always up for a fresh challenge and meeting new and interesting people. It's always fun to wing it and spontaneously figure out what the heck I'm doing on a given assignment. I don't always succeed, but I never give up on striving to do my best. I've been called many times Mr. (add company name) by my fellow temps, and I take that as a huge compliment. It was only fairly recently that I decided to write this book, so most of the stories and jobs are long forgotten. That's OK; there are plenty in the book and more stories to come with my future jobs. I decided not to hire a ghostwriter, as it only seemed fair to write a book from my own perspective—a temp with no writing experience at all. In fact, this could be considered a temp job too, as it's a one-shot deal for me!

What Have I Done?

have inadvertently created a one-of-a-kind job monster. I've witnessed and learned so much on so many levels of various ladders. Much of that knowledge falls into a gray area, where the answers are not always apparent. I have to figure out and reach beyond what I'm supposed to do—and what I'm not supposed to do in the first place. At this point, for example, I can often see precisely what needs to be done right off the bat for any given assignment, whether it's knowing the answers to questions or solutions to problems and arising issues in between. When I'm asked how I know this, I usually just say from experience. Employees understandably want a more solid answer, but I simply don't have one. My true value is often unseen and even misunderstood. There are so many dots that have never been connected completely. It is because of my varied job assignments either ending abruptly or on schedule but with far less time than needed to master a given project. Instead, the dots get quasi connected as soon as the need arises and I'm asked for suggestions. It's pretty much akin to ultra perceptiveness, both personally and professionally.

For example, Company A wants me to create an inventory control program and then the assignment ends before I can finish. Three years will pass and company B wants me to complete a similar program that someone else has already started. Too often employees or bosses have no interest or desire in hearing my input. They'll say, sometimes right in front of me, "He's just a temp. What does he know?" Hours and as long as even months later they'll realize the direction I was trying to point them into was the correct one. How many thousands of man-hours and tens of thousands of dollars were lost because no one listened to some dumb temp? Other times, however, my knowledge is highly coveted and requested and sometimes even demanded. This has led to another kind of temp job—consulting. Let the monster continue to grow in all ways!

Side Note:

CRYSTAL BALL

Even when I was still relatively new at this whole temping thing, I had many assignments already under my belt. Crystal, the temp agency representative, sometimes sent me to rather difficult assignments. She recognized in me the ability to quickly sift through disagreeable clients or jobs and realize success on the other side. Part of it, she knew, was from my experience working varied jobs all the time. The other part was my disposition. I give her a lot of credit for her perceptiveness, as she was pretty young at the time. I appreciate her now as I recall different conversations that we had during her brief time there. I missed her understanding and kindness when she left. A while had passed, and when I called the office for an assignment, Crystal answered. I was shocked but happy that she was back. But, like many of life's good things, it was temporary. She soon moved on to another job field, and once again there was an irreplaceable void in the Boston office.

March 19, 1999; April 6–7, 1999; December 8, 1999; April 14, 2000; July 24, 2000

This was my very first temp job. I didn't know what to expect. I was as excited as I was apprehensive. I was to work here four more times over a more than one-year period. Here I helped to rearrange the offices and cubicles for a governmental agency in Boston whose employees were hearing impaired. Working with one other temp, I had plenty of heavy work ahead moving desks, cabinets, chairs, and other office furniture and equipment. We quickly became comfortable with one another and joked around during breaks. There were dual corridors separated by a wall, and we had to push carts with items on them down these corridors. At one point we did it simultaneously. Just before we headed down our respective corridors, we looked at each other and knew the race was on! We came out pretty much tied, and each of us was happy with the results. Most people like the comfort of familiar surroundings and don't like moving their work areas. Inevitably, many employees were upset that day with the forced relocating of cubicles, cabinets, and the like. Their frustration grew exponentially, since many of the employees weren't able to hear or monitor the situation due to their disability. I wasn't used to being around deaf people and was in no way making fun of them or anyone else for that matter. Still, there were colossal arguments between employees in sign language, and I thought it looked hilarious. The expressions and gestures were so unfamiliar to me, yet so expressive. Some seemed to be vulgar, but I'm only speculating. These arguments would resurface as we moved about the office. In the end I hoped all was well, but there were still plenty of angry faces and gestures to be witnessed. This was certainly an interesting and exciting start to my temp life.

Spontaneous Whiteout

Unknown Date

I worked at a pharmacy in Everett for a bit and one day encountered a most unusual situation. While walking through a snow-covered parking lot with a permanent employee on our way back from a break, the manager pulled up in a car with his brother—who sometimes helped out—riding in the passenger seat. Our manager said something I couldn't quite hear, and the next thing I knew, we were having a two-on-two snowball fight. They jumped out of the car, and it was on. Of course, we had to take it easy on them or risk losing our jobs, so we called it a draw. Afterward, we went inside, warmed up, and dried off while recapping who hit whom and the near misses. I enjoyed the camaraderie with a permanent worker, which is rare in most assignments.

Frozen (Temp)eratures

Unknown Date

'm so glad this was a one-day job. It was at an ice-cream warehouse in Charlestown. My job was to fill customers' orders and pick various flavors and styles from the shelves. The permanent workers assisted me with their forklifts to reach the shelves that were sky-high. I remember looking up and thinking, *Man, if this ever fell*...It might as well have been concrete; it weighed a ton. And there were a few close calls. The pushcarts and forklifts weren't made for the extreme cold, especially if you had any kind of weight bearing down on them. They were trembling just like we were. I didn't have much notice for the job, so I grabbed my best boots, which were steel-toe. Big mistake. It didn't take long before I couldn't feel my toes. I just laughed at the irony that steel-toe boots were supposed to protect your toes. Here I was about to lose them. I sat down at one of the tables during a break in the lunch-room, talking with some employees. The next thing I knew, they were dealing drugs right in front of me. What were they thinking? They knew nothing of me.

Was it not possible that I would call the cops? I was right there in the middle of it all, so I could have been looked at as an active participant. All these thoughts ran through my head, even though I acted casual and said nothing. They must have been too lazy to make an effort to do the transaction while they were alone. Maybe they simply didn't care or really did have brain freeze from being permanently exposed to such bone-chilling temperatures. I finished out the day and then went outside into the summer sizzle, which felt as hot as the sun with the contrast. I desperately needed it to thaw out my toes, so I was happy to be in the heat and to be on my way to the next adventure.

Anger That Quickly Floated Away

Unknown Company and Date

I worked with many temps at a company that sold water-filtration systems. The manager, a rather zany guy, would assume different characters depending on whom or what he was talking about. Just like a character actor, he completely transformed himself for any role a situation called for. The only difference was that he was portraying himself each time! During one meeting, he stood in front of us, upset at certain pressing issues. At the end of his speech, he angrily launched a piece of paper that was in his hands. It floated in the air as if it didn't have a care in the world. For what seemed like an eternity, it twisted and turned like an aerial acrobat. It finally ended up in its final resting place a few feet away from him. His anger instantly became a sulk as he looked at it and then simply walked away. Paper one, manager zero.

Unknown Date

At a bank in Malden, one of my responsibilities was to sort out a customer's cash deposits into separate bags. Each bag was to be processed at a later time and place. The deposits came in different-sized envelopes, ranging from tiny envelopes that would fit a few bills to huge ones that could hold wads of cash and even some checks. It would take two people to sort. One person would determine which bag the envelopes were to go in, while the other person held the bags wide open. The bags were cumbersome and probably polyester or nylon, so when we tried to hold them open, the mouth would flop around. It was difficult, then, for the holder to keep it wide open. It was also difficult to manage when the weight kept changing due to the constant adding of envelopes. I have only one speed—maximum—which came in handy when I sorted out the envelopes. The faster I sorted, the easier for the bag holder. I worked with different employees on varying days, and they all agreed that it made sense for me to be the sorter. Weeks later

I happened to be paired up with a petite young girl new to this particular job. I showed her what to do, and she was ready. I started whipping the envelopes as usual into the bags. Suddenly, the girl started screaming loudly, as if she were being murdered! I abruptly stopped the sorting to see what the problem was. Evidently, I had scared the hell out of her with my lightning speed. I didn't ask her, but she might have likened it to an assault or something that she may have experienced in her life. One of the envelopes had cut her hand slightly as it buzzed its way by, so that must have added to her horror. I got her a Band-Aid and apologized for what happened. She still looked traumatized as we continued working, but this time very slowly. Ah, the effect I have on people.

Unknown Date

worked for one day at a furniture delivery company that rented and sold used furniture. I rearranged and staged some furniture orders in their warehouse for a few hours. After I loaded some trucks, it was time to hit the road for some deliveries. I was sent to work with a mountain of a man. I'm not a small man, but compared to him I definitely was. Where do they get these giant guys who are perfect for the job? I never see them around much. Without them these jobs would probably simply not get done. I give them much credit as they bust their asses on a daily basis. That day we hit many locations with deliveries but also had some furniture rental pickups. Although he lifted and carried most of the heavy stuff, I assisted him with all of the pickups and deliveries, one of which sticks out most in my mind. As he descended a flight of stairs with a gigantic couch thrown over his shoulder, I remember thinking how huge his hands were and how effortless he seemed to do the incredible things that he did. He obviously didn't need help, but I had to at least offer.

Of course he declined. So I ended up tiptoeing behind him like a pillow fairy clutching a few pillows as if that was any help. I felt emasculated to say the least. I hope no one saw us.

Unknown Company and Date

It was rare not to know which job I'd be assigned on a given day, so this one was unexpected. I showed up at my company's office in Malden thinking this was an indoor job. Little did I know that my assignment called for shoveling snow at many remote locations. I often wear only thin jackets because the cold doesn't really bother me much; plus, I'm usually not outdoors for long intervals. As fate would have it, I'd be braving a large snowstorm chock-full of whipping winds—totally unprepared. Along with my thin jacket, which was really only a heavy shirt, I wore only a pair of sneakers and khakis. I desperately needed gloves, a hat/ski mask, a scarf, and a real jacket for this undertaking. But off I went into the frozen tundra. I shoveled frantically, which created a nice, warm sweat. However, stopping even for a minute was out of the question. I wasn't keen to be a Popsicle. I thawed out several times since I was carted off to the different locations in my contact's cozy, heated pickup truck. By the end of the day, I was fully thawed out, and all was well with the world again.

Thomas the Train

Unknown Company and Date

''ve worked several times over the years with one particular temp. Once, while we were moving heavy boxes, he told me that this pile we were moving was one of many. With glee I responded, "Bring it on!" He was quite impressed with my attitude and joked that I was "Thomas the Train" since my name is Thomas after all, and I intended to *choo-choo* right through any pile of boxes that I could find. As it turns out, he was right!

Unknown Company and Date

A bunch of us temps worked for several days at a conference, where we moved signs from room to room indicating which meeting would be in what particular room and when. We also greeted people and distributed information packets. But the humorous job, at least I thought, was holding up flash cards in the back of the room to indicate how much time was left for the presenter of a certain session. Sometimes we would switch up employees midmeeting for breaks and such, so we'd often come in missing half the subject matter. Not that we were supposed to gain anything from these meetings; we were there just to flash signs. Still, I like to learn when given the opportunity. My mind did wander those times when I had just entered the room and missed half the meeting. I'd think of all the possible funny messages that could have been written on those flash cards. I could have custom written them given a particular meeting's subject or the way the presenter looked, acted, and so on. The shock on a presenter's face would have been priceless!

Good Night, Beantown

Unknown Company and Date

I was supposed to be helping with the moving of hospital beds at a Boston hospital. When I showed up, I saw all the beds to be transported, but not the company representative. I waited an extra hour to be sure and then left. This was on a Saturday, so when I called my company Monday they told me that it was fine and paid me for the day. Good night, all!

One-Day Job? Or Not...

Unknown Company and Date

I was dispatched to a lawyer's office for one day of labor. I arrived at the location promptly and met with the receptionist. First, she had me move five legal-sized boxes from one corner of the small greeting area to the other. When I asked her what she wanted me to do next, she said that was it and paid me for the day. *Great*, I thought. *Less than one minute of work for a day of pay.* I wondered if it was office politics or if the boxes were too heavy for her. Maybe it wasn't appropriate to ask a lawyer to move them. I guess I'll never know, but it was a good day—or, rather, a good minute. Maybe they were just flush with cash. In any case, that's got to be some sort of record for the shortest temp job in history.

Clocked Out?

Unknown Company and Date

This one-day job employed four temps. It was an unusual assignment, as it was helping to move out a gentleman from his apartment in Boston. This was my first and only experience working for a nonbusiness (unless it was under the guise of one). Anyway, all went well loading the truck, until the end of the day when a gigantic sleeper couch wouldn't fit in the elevator. I couldn't even guess the weight or how they got it in the apartment in the first place. He asked us to carry it down several flights of stairs, and each of us would have a crisp, new twenty-dollar bill for our efforts. We jumped at the chance for the extra money and the satisfaction of a completed job/challenge. I guess he must have checked with our agency and discovered it wasn't acceptable for us to perform amazing and dangerous feats under contract. Instead, he paid us our twenty bucks under the table. With Boston's old and narrow staircases, the couch barely fit down, even as we navigated and carefully maneuvered it. At one juncture, the bottom edge came down like a hammer on a nail—right on top of my head. I was stunned to say the least, but fortunately one of the guys had a solid enough hold on it, which is why I'm here to write these words. Some years have passed since then, so I guess there's no drain bramage.

Orange Containment

Unknown Company and Date

This single-day job consisted of clearing out an employee's cubicle and other small cabinets and closets into a moving truck. I presume he was going to another company location and wasn't fired, since it was his company that hired me. After a hard day's work in the summer heat, he offered me a six-pack of orange soda that he'd had in his cubicle. I accepted and hopped on the train, headed home. I soon realized that the plastic ring that holds the cans in place was tricky to hold with one hand. Not to mention the train was full, so I had to hold on to the bar with my other hand. As fate would have it, out they came— one can to the left, one to the right. I held on to two, but the others scattered. Surprisingly, no one got hit, and none of the cans exploded. I scooped them up and ended up drinking them all when I got off the train, after the fizzing settled. Delicious thanks.

Unknown Company and Date

This one-day job required two of us temps, but only I showed up. My job was in Medford and entailed unloading floor tiles from a truck for a sub-contractor who would eventually lay them down for a new store. I didn't realize what I was in for, though. There was an eighteen-wheeler full front to back of the tiles. It was ominous with two workers, but alone? There were no carts, hand trucks, or lifts. I had to scramble up the backside of the truck and lift each tile box just to hop back down with it, then across the sidewalk and deep into the store. Each box was pretty heavy at around sixty to seventy pounds. I had to repeat this over and over again with every lift seemingly heavier and heavier. To make matters worse, the wind chill was well below zero; when I came off the truck onto the sidewalk, the wind nearly knocked me over. Soon into it, I was soaked with sweat, and every time I came off that truck I was flash frozen. Damn that other temp for not showing up! I was in pretty good shape, though I desperately needed water. I wasn't interested in food at all, so I trudged across the parking lot to a market to guzzle water and bring a sufficient amount back with me. After all this was done, I thought it was over—but no. Out the rear door was a huge Dumpster that the contractors and subcontractors were using for building material discards. I was instructed to maximize space by flattening the debris inside so they could add more. I leapt atop the heap and navigated my way through all sorts of gnarly situations without any equipment, gloves, or proper footwear. I had some splinters and close calls with nails through the feet, but all ended well. I managed to finish after many hours and went home to shower, but my body was still shaking from all the effort it took. Something different I guess, huh?

Unknown Company and Date

worked for one day at this company and directly with my contact. We moved heavy furniture up tall flights of stairs, which was difficult enough, but the temperature was over one hundred degrees with very high humidity. The job was partly outside, depending on the task, and there were no fans or air conditioning on the inside. I gave my contact a lot of credit because it was pretty unusual for me to work with employees of the company that hired me, as it was almost always for them. We were soaked head to toe, but it certainly wasn't raining. In the end he decided to tip me for my effort. Though it was unusual, I happily accepted. The bills were completely wet as well, and when I went to the store for a drink shortly after, I was shocked to see that the coins in my pocket had turned rusty! That's the only time I ever remember that happening. With all of the brutal jobs that I've done, it's surprising. It must have been the right combination of pennies, nickels, dimes, and quarters and maybe even keys.

Unknown Company and Date

Shortly after 9/11, I worked one late-night assignment and returned early the next morning to finish. It was with two other temps and our contact. There was to be advertising between local train stops on Boston's T system, specifically the red line in Cambridge and Boston. It's a unique way of advertising in that there were plastic slats angling at passengers in different positions along the tracks. Looking at them straight on, you can't see anything. But when you reach a certain speed or angle in these dark train tunnels, an ad appears almost like stop-go animation. Our job was to count the number of people who got on and off the train at specific times and stops. It was definitely a ridiculous and suspicious-looking activity as the four of us broke up into two teams to cover a particular car on the train. With our walkie-talkies and our handheld counters, we'd try to whisper our counts to each other in an attempt to avoid annoying or upsetting the train patrons. Sometimes we'd use hand signals to relay counts if there were no walkie-talkie signals in a particular tunnel. But the more subtle we were, the more suspicious we looked. We most definitely had a lot of curious smiles, but others demanded to know what we were doing and threatened to call 911. We told them in the quickest way we could while still being courteous. We were still trying to relay the counts, and there were many quick train stops without much time to relay the information. Our contact was from the UK and had already done this here and elsewhere, so thankfully he had his spiel to the patrons down pat. Prior to 9/11, few people would've noticed or cared. Another interesting assignment for the books, though.

Look Out Down Below!

Unknown Company and Date

For this one-day job, I worked with the same temp as I did on a previous job, which had been fun. On this day, though, we worked in a six- or seven-story office building in Cambridge and performed light industrial duties such as moving desks and bolting down cabinets. This particular company's office was located on the top floor. On their balcony, however, was a huge picnic table that we were told to toss over the edge! What the heck? A professional company said *what*? We were serving the clients' needs and didn't want to hesitate. Still, our eyes locked with a knowing look. We sent our contact to the ground-level area to make sure the coast was clear since there were so many people and cars coming and going in the parking lot. In the meantime, we discussed the liability of such an action and all the potential consequences. Well, we got the nod from below, and then came the old heave-ho and *smash*—right to the ground. To our relief it was anticlimactic but fun at least. Afterward, we stacked the pieces into possible firewood and called it a day.

Unknown Company and Date

I worked for a few days in East Boston at a photography company that specialized in holiday-themed shoots. I remember thinking how strange it was to be taking photos of Thanksgiving or Christmas plates and cutlery in the middle of summer. Although they did have an assortment of holiday toys as well for their catalog, it was mostly dinnerware, bowls, and candy dishes. As some of the photos were being shot, it seemed the photographers stopped short of telling the objects to smile for the camera, or to look sexy or something. That's because of the pause between the final setup of the object and the snap of the picture. That comical angle amused me probably because I was new; I doubt if the photographers saw the humor. When handling the more shiny objects, we wore these cumbersome gloves in order to avoid leaving fingerprints. Even the minutest amount of skin oil would show up in the pictures. With my gloves on, I had a hard time adjusting some of the ornamental bowls as well as the forks and knives. Sometimes I would try to nudge them with my fingers to achieve the desired angle, but of course the prints showed up. We used fine cloths to wipe them clean, but we'd end up moving the delicate objects. It was a continual process of set down, adjust, and then wipe—sort of like going to the bathroom.

The Auctioneer Was Going
about a Mile a Minute

Unknown Company and Date

With a few other temps, I was sent to an estate auction held at an exclusive Boston hotel. I was the auctioneer's right-hand man. During the preview, he was pretty busy answering questions and familiarizing himself with the many high-priced items that were to be sold. He was very good at what he did, I came to find out. I looked at all of the items too, but naming them was a different story. During the auction itself, I was to write down the item's number, name, and description. It seemed like a piece of cake. I was wrong. He started off quickly as the words flew right from his tongue. I was in trouble. I managed to jot down some of the item names, but the descriptions were another story. If only it could have been recorded; then there would have been plenty of time to log everything in. Couldn't this have been done prior to the auction? But what do I know. I struggled but did the best I could, hoping it wouldn't be useless drivel. When I could, I whispered to him to clarify certain words or phrases for me. I certainly didn't have many chances since he was going so darn fast! The phrase that capped my confusing day was *oriental Isfahan*. He might as well have been speaking a different language. I learned later that Isfahan is a city in Iran; he was offering up an exclusive Persian rug. I'd hoped he was satisfied, but I never found out. I also wondered how another temp would've handled it. My head did finally stop spinning afterward. The auctioneer was even busier tying up loose ends, so I never really got a chance to get clarification or feedback. I really wanted to, as I rarely leave a job dissatisfied.

Unknown Company and Date

I was fresh off a long-term temp office job when I got the call. I was going to work at a golf course in Melrose—*yes!* It was the very next day. Going from a cubicle one day to the great outdoors the next was exhilarating. That it was raining didn't matter. In fact, I sort of welcomed a physically demanding job in the elements. I didn't want to be well done in the sun. Soon after I met with my contact, we were flying down the forest path in a golf cart. What a thrill for me; the timing was perfect. There were some other temps there, and our job for the next several days was to help an irrigation company. We basically changed the underground pipes from old metal ones to new space-age plastic ones. I had a lot of fun digging around in such a beautiful setting. When I got there, the project was almost over. Still, I enjoyed working on my hands and knees in the mud and muck, breathing in the fresh summer air.

Unknown Company and Date

I worked for one day for a private contractor in a home improvement store that had its own particular display of products that needed to be updated and organized. Most of the day had us—mostly me—removing the price and product information stickers off the front edge of the shelves. The stickers had been there for several years, so removing them was tough. They gave me razor blades and cleaning fluids with cloths. Only the razors really worked, so that's what I used. Cleanly pulling a sticker off wasn't possible, so, piece by piece, the stickers were carefully sliced and then pulled off by fingernails and then by fingers. I had to be careful not to cut the trademark-orange shelf edges, as it really was noticeable. Also, we relabeled the shelves, but on different sections of the display, as fate would have it. I had to squat in the most peculiar positions to get the right angle of the blade onto the shelves. It probably looked funny to passersby. It was physically grueling to partake in such a task as I contorted like a pretzel throughout the project. Gloves would have hindered any progress, so I finished at the end of the day with some blood loss and a few missing fingerprints.

Unknown Company and Date

I worked for an evening with one other temp in a restaurant and lounge in Everett, where function rooms are rented out for a variety of occasions. In this case, it was for a hypnotist who professed to offer the cure for weight loss and smoking cessation in a one-stop shopping arena. He stationed us in the front of the room to register people and, when the session was over, to sell his wares. It was pretty expensive to get in at around $75, but some attendees had discounts as there were flyers around town advertising the special offers. The room was full to capacity, and some people paid only to have to stand. During his opening speech, he made it clear that he'd use the exact same techniques for weight loss *and* smoking cessation. That, for me, was a red flag. He was also very outgoing and deliberate with his use of words. At certain points he instructed the attendees to close their eyes as he employed his brainwashing techniques. Then he would tiptoe over to us, still carrying the microphone so the attendees thought he was still in front of them, and mouth instructions to us temps. He wanted to make sure that all the piles of cash were well accounted for and to remind us about the selling that was to come afterward. His facial expressions were hilarious but seemed insincere; he was really being careful so no one would notice, but naturally some of the attendees peeked and probably rolled their eyes. As he moved along, trying to hypnotize everyone, I couldn't help but laugh at his words and phrases, which sounded so ridiculous. He had some people lying on the floor as if they were dead and then snapped his fingers to awaken them, like a healer would. When the hour-long session was over, he rallied everyone over to purchase his CDs and DVDs to further help them along in their battles. Some came over and demanded a refund, which he readily gave; then he pushed them out quickly to limit the damage. Others left without saying anything but did have angry looks on them. Most were satisfied though, and a lot of them did spend plenty of money on the products. I guess when you desperately need a change, you're willing to try anything. Also, how could they really be sure if his hypnotizing worked until they went back to their own reality, for a few days at least? While I saw the whole thing as a big hoax, I do hope some attendees were helped.

We're Just Making a Phone Call

Unknown Company and Date

I t was either 2000 or 2001, when cell-phone use was still relatively new. For this two-day job, our contact had me and another temp go inside certain Boston skyscrapers and other structures to test a particular cell-phone model's signal strength. Some of the buildings had prearranged plans that were agreed upon by our contact's company, which gave us free rein to explore certain corners for testing. My favorite location was the FleetCenter, which is now the TD Banknorth Garden. Having access on this quiet day and simply taking in the atmosphere while looking up at the Celtics and Bruins championship banners was refreshing. We walked around and tested all over the place, including the nosebleed sections all the way down to the front-row seats. How lucky we were to have the freedom to roam and look behind the scenes at such a historic place. Realizing that many people would never have the chance, I soaked up as much as possible; Boston is such a huge sports city. For other structures, however, this was not the case. Those were the fun buildings where we had to covertly test the phones in random corners of certain floors. There were also staircases and elevators to conquer. We generally roamed around, much to the dismay of some security personnel. I don't remember if it was after 9/11, but security was strict, in some cases booting us out. Because our contact had done this job before, he knew which buildings would be a security problem. I'm sure it would have been a logistical nightmare to have to contact every structure ahead of time. It seemed he enjoyed the challenge of a successful phone test without anyone finding out. Nevertheless, we temps made the most of the excitement since it was the closest we'd ever get to being real spies. The buildings we entered had some curious onlookers. We started out in a group and were given instructions on where to go within the vicinity. As we fanned out, the onlookers watched, as if these cell phones were futuristic gadgets and would make us levitate or something while we tested them. Of course they were disappointed, but that's what you get for being nosy.

Unknown Company and Date

This job was in Cambridge and lasted for one day and had several of us temps in attendance. The company had an upcoming project. All we had to do was carry in tons of metal pipes and all different shapes and sizes of sheet metal and various other metal fittings. It was all brought into a large basement room, mostly through a set of double doors. For the longer pieces, we used the basement windows because that was the only way they would fit. It was funny to see these guys laying on the ground and jamming metal awkwardly through the narrow windows. Some of the guys would just throw the metal they lugged onto the pile on the ground instead of placing it. Because of the room's acoustics it was ear-shattering, reverberating through my soul and the building. The others didn't seem bothered by it, though.

The Birds (Cars, Actually) and the Bees

Unknown Company and Date

This single-day job was an unusual road-trip experience. My contact Mike and I drove probably over two hundred miles that day to deliver a very heavy stair-climbing machine. Apparently, the machine itself was used to carry large items up or down the stairs. Maybe because certain companies didn't have freight elevators, they needed to walk heavy items up or down. When we arrived at our destination we attempted to carry up a (probably empty) soda-vending machine with our contraption. We loaded it just fine, but once we started up the stairs the trouble began. The wooden stairs started to crumble. We quickly stopped the behemoth and brought it back down the few stairs without it getting damaged or us killed. Mike called his company for some guidance. We ended up just packing our machine into our truck and left. The soda machine stayed put on the original level; I never found out anything else since it was my only day there. My guess is that Mike's company not only didn't get paid but also had to pay to repair the couple of steps we shattered. Meanwhile, since it was a beautiful summer day, we had the windows rolled down on the highway. Mike mentioned that bees always seemed to find their way to his midsection on road trips. It was always him and never the passenger, he explained. Shortly after that, what do you know? *Splat!* A direct hit in his gut! The bee bounced onto the floor, and he stepped on it. "See? I told you!" Mike said, exasperated. "It never fails!" I just sat back and relaxed the rest of the drive back as I knew there was no bee on my radar. *Ahh*.

Silence Speaks Volumes

Unknown Company and Date

Once, I had a one-day job that required me to move office furniture for my contact, a woman. She sort of shadowed me since she had the normal indecision most people have during moves. After all, one never really knows exactly how a certain piece of furniture will look in a given location until it's actually there. The day progressed as normal until I carried a desk up some stairs for her—when suddenly out from the drawer pops a condom! It was new and wrapped and fell on the ground between us. We just gave each other a knowing smirk as she bent to pick it up. Not a word was spoken by either of us.

Unknown Company and Date

guess you could call this a job, even though the pleasure was certainly all mine. It was only for a day, but
I wouldn't have minded if the job had lasted forever
(or—dare I say it?—was permanent). I'd had an idea
of what was to come. Still, I wondered what I gotten myself into. Inside the medical office, I had to put
around my penis what amounted to an expensive rub-
ber band fastened to a string that was attached to a
machine. I put it on, very carefully, and was instructed
to watch pornography. I was thinking that boy I hate
this job. The researcher happened to be superhot and
wore a tight short skirt with high heels. I hope it just
happened to be her style and was totally independent
of the study. And get this, if I didn't like the movie
choice, I could let her know and she'd put in a different movie for me. *Does it get any better than this?*
I wondered. She changed the movies from another
room and communicated through speakers only, unfortunately. This was around 2001 or 2002, and the
movies were from the early eighties—not that I would

know or anything. When I mentioned this, she told me they would soon get newer clips, and whether or not they were old or new movies had nothing to do with their research needs. I didn't really ask many questions since I was in such a state of bliss. I also didn't want to bog down their research. What we subjects had to do was put the ring around the center of our wieners and watch XXX movies, without masturbating whatsoever. I don't know how many other subjects participated as we each had a private room. Nor do I know if females participated in the study. From what I gathered, the researchers needed to measure the growth of subjects with their hands totally free. Size didn't matter—only a subject's increase in size while visually stimulated or excited. The researcher started and stopped us intermittently by pausing actual movie clips, sometimes without our consent. The screen would darken momentarily, just long enough to get you down, if you know what I mean. If this is not the most noteworthy—dare I call it exciting? (at least for guys)—temp job of all time, then I want to hear the one that is! Needless to say, the temp jobs went downhill from there.

The Train to Nowhere

Unknown Date

I worked for a few weeks at a pharmacy in Medford. The chain has since been bought out. Some other temps were there as well as other permanent workers. It was a brand-new store, and we were all doing jobs from *A* to *Z* to ensure a successful grand opening. During a break one day with one of my fellow temps, we went outside toward the back of the building since we were working near the rear of the store anyway. As we chatted, a train pulled into the stop that was about fifty feet away from us. We looked on as the passengers departed and boarded. Our conversation changed as he told me with such a yearning in his eyes that he would love to go on the train that minute. I shared his desire to feed our wanderlust. It didn't matter to us where it was going but just to ride a train to wherever and forget our worries while gazing out the window at the passing of life.

Unknown Date

A few dozen of us temps were mobilized to work for a ticket scalping company for the day in Worcester. Each one of us was given a particular amount of money to stand in line and buy Madonna tickets for an upcoming show. We were given specific rows in certain sections to purchase and made sure not to stray from those areas and instead hold on to the cash if they weren't available. Of course, the scalping company knew exactly which tickets in a row/section not to buy since they might have to eat the cost. I didn't prefer doing this job since it was unfair to everyone else who wanted a good seat at face value, me included. After each temp's turn in line, he or she would go to the end of the line and repeat the process since there were limits on the number of tickets you could buy per person. Our contacts figured that the people selling the tickets would forget our faces, see a different seller, or just wouldn't care during our repeat performances, which is exactly what happened. The ticket prices were already very high, but to legally scalp them at an even more outrageous price didn't sit well with me. (I'm not sure why it's legal for a business to do it but not an individual.) I felt like scalping our contacts (just kidding!).

Choosing to Go Back to Prison

Unknown Date

Before I ventured into the temp world, I had a permanent career. I choose not to name the field, company, etc. for my own privacy reasons. Seemingly out of nowhere, my manager of many years spoke very harshly to me. It was definitely uncalled for. I had never given anyone at work or otherwise even a remote reason to speak to me in such a demeaning, negative manner. I mulled over his poor treatment of me during the rest of the day and decided that was it. I finished out the day and retrieved my belongings. I quietly said my good-byes to some close coworkers and then went up to HR for my exiting paperwork. I remember walking through an alley on my way home. I just raised my arms and smiled at the freedom of it all. I never could have imagined this situation would or could have come up on the same route just that morning. Something in me said it was time to go, although I'm not sure I could ever pinpoint it. Eight years, six months, and five days is what it ended up being. I joke about it today as being prison time. It wasn't until after I left and some time had passed that it seemed to be just that. Don't get me wrong. The job was fine, and I didn't have any complaints. That is why I was there for so long. But something about cutting the cord is so liberating, which only now I realize. This applies to all facets of life; in many situations cord cutting can be advantageous.

A temp assignment came up at my former "prison" location a few years later. When I left originally, I vowed never to enter the building again. But the job was only for a day, so as a private joke to myself I agreed to do it. Although it was in a different department, I recognized some of the employees. A few asked me if I used to work there because I looked familiar. I told them no and this was my first time there. It was definitely surreal to go back to the "prison", but the experience was worth it. Just knowing that I was there to work only one day was spectacular. For some reason I felt badly for the regular employees I'd seen there for years when I was there, who were still there during my visit. Maybe they too never realized that there is so much out there to experience in life, personally and professionally. I hope they're content, though. Let freedom ring.

Surprise, Surprise

Unknown Date

I worked a one-day job that had me doing lawn care and generally sprucing up a college campus in Brookline. I went about my day's activities. I mowed the lawns and changed barrels. My next task was to vacuum the hallways, floor by floor, in the campus dorms. I had just begun when suddenly a female college student walked from her room to the shower area with only a towel around her. Then another girl did the same thing, and so on. They couldn't care less that I was there; they casually strolled by as if I were just another roommate. I figured that there were probably always guys there doing my job. Still, I was surprised—pleasantly surprised time and again. Oh, the things I do for my company.

Unbelievable or Not?
That Is the Question

Unknown Date

I worked with a bunch of temps at a bookstore in an upscale Boston mall. It was a brand-new location so much work was to be done. During my break I sat on a bench outside the store, directly across from an escalator. I looked up and down came a stunning woman. I was curious to see what kind of man could snag this type of lady, so I glanced behind her. It was none other than Roger Clemens—unbelievable. He was in town playing against our beloved Red Sox for the hated Yankees. But, of course, he is a Boston sports icon and still well respected around these parts. After my break I mentioned this to a coworker who said it's *not* unbelievable that I saw him; Roger was just a man and not a god or something. I acknowledged that he was only a man. I think I was misunderstood since my coworker thought I was trying to put Roger on a pedestal. All I said in my excitement was the word unbelievable—one word, and now we're having a philosophical discussion about gods?

Dancing Here...And There

Unknown Dates

I worked at a certain bank several times over the years in Boston. This particular time was during a bank merger, so some desks, chairs, file folders, and so on needed to be packed up and transported to a different city by movers. I worked for one lady named Maureen, but she did loan me out to others as we went along. From time to time, she would randomly break out in a dance of some sort while humming a tune. She was an older lady, which somehow made it more interesting. She was very vibrant and positive about life, which is why I have fond memories of her. She'd loved the job I was doing so much that she asked me to unpack her in the new city. Because it was so far away, she offered to have me on the clock the moment I left my house. I agreed and once we got into the new place her dancing continued, much to my pleasure.

I did my own sort of dancing another time when I worked at this bank. There was a huge vault-like room full to the brim with bank files. The file boxes were scattered all over the place as if they'd been placed any old way. It was a monumental mess, to say the least. Some of the permanent employees there were very unmotivated and unhelpful. I and a few other temps were there for about a week. I came up with a game plan on how to best conquer the mess. The bank had one of those movable aisle-rolling file and storage shelving systems. Having the rolling aisles was critical to our success. We danced around the scattered boxes on the floors and cabinets and then spun back around to reorganize them onto the shelves on the aisles. There were already file boxes on the shelves, so we integrated the newer boxes to the best of our ability with the little bit of information we had. I felt badly for the employees who would need certain files in the future; it would be pretty difficult to locate them. I hoped we helped in a big way, though it was so hard to tell. Trying out different dance moves was fun at least. Don't expect to see these moves at any club or gathering, though.

Unknown Date

I helped another lady unpack in the same office since Maureen loaned me out to her. Not only did I unpack, but I also helped her with interior designing. We strategically placed all sorts of flower displays, paintings, vases, and various other odds and ends in a most extravagant manner. She was drop-dead gorgeous, which made it all the more pleasant for me. She wanted a lamp placed a certain way on the top of a large end table. I would have done it, but she went up quickly—miniskirt, high heels, and all. She asked me to hand her the lamp, but as I did I had to look down; everything was on display for me to see. She kept talking to me seemingly unaware. Ah, life as a temp isn't always tough.

Whoever Said There Is No Free Lunch?

Unknown Date

During a stint at a bank one week, an employee told me to help myself to the lunch that was being served in the conference room. I helped myself for the next several days as well, enjoying all sorts of fine fare, all the while talking and mingling with executives. As it turns out, I wasn't in the bank's conference room. I'd been in an adjacent room booked by many companies in the building! Where is that employee who told me about this in the first place? He could have gotten me canned, and the bank could have been embarrassed, too. Since I gave the impression that I belonged in the conference room, everyone assumed I belonged. The person you project is the person you are, right? It's funny recalling my nonchalance, helping myself to the high-quality food and drink. Delicious thanks, again.

The Exchange That Wasn't Kosher

Unknown Dates

I frequently worked as a mystery diner at a Jewish college cafeteria in Waltham. My first time there brought a little misunderstanding. I'd chosen my food for lunch and was ready to pay when the cashier said, "Kosher?" I was so focused on my undercover duties, such as looking for cleanliness, promptness of service, and so on, that I froze. In my preoccupation, I'd asked, "What's the difference?" He started to explain the difference between kosher and non-kosher foods when I blurted out, "I knew that, but I meant what's the difference in price?" Once he told me, I paid and was on my way. It was a weird mix-up for both of us. I'm not sure if he thought I was challenging him, but it ranks as another unusual experience from my temp-life files.

The Muffin Man

Several Companies and Dates

I worked with one temp, Jack McSomething, on and off for about two years. He was quite an interesting character who was also a thief. Every time I saw him at a particular assignment, he was up to no good. The most expensive item I saw him steal was a very large, thick hardcover book that was set out on display in a posh office. I'm not sure what the subject matter was. He just took it and put it under his jacket. The cubed ledge area it came from was now glaringly empty. The other display areas looked normal with their adorn-ments, which only drew attention to the empty ledge. I just cringed because it wasn't even the end of the work day. Someone easily could have noticed which put our jobs and our company in jeopardy. I'm no rat but was often put in that situation with Jack. He stole several items from the different companies that we worked for. Once he even unplugged a phone and took it off the wall! I couldn't call the police if I wanted to. At the end of one workday, a permanent employee had set down a bag of a few dozen muffins and said he'd be right back. The muffins happened to be near the door on our way out, so Jack just grabbed them like a sack of toys from Santa Claus and threw the bag of muffins over his shoulder as he went on his way. We happened to be walking in the same direction, so I walked with him, expecting the worst. But no one ever shouted out to us. Maybe we were out of sight by the time the guy came back looking for it. Who knows? I definitely thought about reporting him each time, but I was concerned that he'd say I was a part of it too, as his defense. I should have let my company know or at least told one of our contacts. I just wanted to do the best job I could for our contacts with no drama involved. If it came down to it, I would've told the truth. He was an older guy who worked here and there to supplement his social security and whatever other income and benefits he had. He shared that information with me as well as his other life stories. Maybe he wasn't always a thief. Perhaps he was getting desperate for the extra income and sold the items. I really don't know. He was a pretty nice guy, and when he'd tell me stories, they would often begin with "I'm sixty-four years old…" I didn't see him for quite some time; still, we picked up right where we left off, with both the thefts and the stories. But this time he began, "I'm sixty-six years old…"

August 5, 2001

This one-day job had several of us temps overseeing children's activities in an amusement-park setting in Boston. The vast majority of activities included hastily erected rides since it was a one-day event. For this assignment, we were given too much responsibility. As we scrambled to learn how to operate various rides, I realized the danger these kids were put in. It was in the inner city, and I doubted the budget would allow for a better situation. We rotated among the different rides to cover breaks, and then it was my turn to man an inflatable bounce house. However, being the cheap version, this one had no walls. I'm not sure why they're legal but, in any case, I monitored the kids carefully. With so many kids hopping on it simultaneously, it's not surprising that one of them flew off it like Superman. I caught him in the nick of time, before he slammed headfirst into the ground. He just laughed it off and hopped on it again, like that was part of the ride or something. What if I was petite and couldn't handle the catch? Or, what if I hadn't been there at that moment? Did this happen often? A flood of questions deluged my mind. I just shook my head and was glad that plenty of kids had a lot of fun that day.

Kids' Fair That Was Unfair: Part 2

August 18, 2001

I took a drive to the suburbs of Boston for another one-day amusement park-type job. It was less than two weeks after my first one, and I'd hoped it would be a little fairer this time around. It was a private company's party catering to the kids of their employees. So I was given my purple T-shirt with the company logo on it, and off I went. The temps staffed the eight games in which the kids could win prizes. Since it was company paid, the kids would line up again and again without the worry of paying, until they were satisfied with their winnings. But one kid in particular was determined to win every single time and refused to stop playing, even at the expense of other kids who were crying or being brushed aside. Parents rarely came over, so we had to bribe him with prizes. It was a beautiful day though, and we made sure all the children had the maximum amount of fun and all of the prizes were given out.

September 13, 2001; October 9, 2001; October 11, 2001; October 18, 2001; November 27, 2001; November 7, 2002; November 13–14, 2002; November 20, 2002

worked at a health company eight times over a one-year period. We would set up shop in various colleges to administer immunizations—mostly for meningitis, both bacterial and viral. Many were first-year students still in their teens who were away from home for the first time, and there was no more hand-holding from Mom or Dad. As the students lined up and filled out the appropriate paperwork, the tension grew at a fever pitch. Most fidgeted and talked, probably because they were bored or needed a distraction. Some cringed at the sight of needles and others from the pain itself. One girl, though, took the cake. Just prior to her shot, she screamed like a siren from a low pitch to a piercing screech. Then she cried. But the shot itself was uneventful, and all turned out well. I doubted if this helped students who were next in line, though. Sometimes students would just faint, almost always before the needle prick. It wasn't as if they'd had a bad reaction to the shot. The mind-body relationship is quite interesting, huh?

Unknown Company and Date

worked for a couple of weeks or so in a shipping/ receiving and sorting area for a small travel company in Boston. Prior to working here, I'd give bone-crushing handshakes when introducing myself. After all, society views a firm handshake as a sign of strong character. My societal view changed at this company, though. When I met and shook hands with an employee I'd be working with, he grimaced and let out a hellacious scream, to my shock and embarrassment. I apologized and all was well, except for his hand. I'd never gotten that reaction before—usually just grunts and distorted faces, along with comments like "Wow! You have a strong grip." Some even shook their hand around, testing it to see if it still worked. Although I have always tried to shake hands with a strong grip to show the greatest of character, this job experience changed my mind. I now give soft-to-medium handshakes. I guess my character's in question.

All Hail to the Union: Part 1

Unknown Date

I was sent here to assist a small company that had its own display of products for the upcoming grand opening of a baby clothes and toys chain store location in Medford. I was to help put up shelves and stock products. But it was a one-day job that lasted zero hours. As my two contacts were giving me instructions, we were rudely interrupted by a union representative who shouted, "If you don't leave, I'm going to smack you in the face." *Joy*, I thought. I went outside with my contacts and they apologized to me. They were going to find out how to proceed but, in the meantime, they let me go with pay for the day. There is so much red tape and so many different kinds of unions. It must be difficult for the companies that have to deal with these types of issues when they simply want to get a job done. While unions are good for many reasons, they also sometimes promote laziness, as I've seen firsthand countless times and assignments.

All Hail to the Union: Part 2

October 30, 2008

’ve had many run-ins with all types of unions, as I mentioned in part 1. This time was more ridiculous than usual, though. Some of us temps were deployed to work for a company that was providing audio/visual support for an event to be held at a Boston hotel. Our job was to unload a tractor-trailer full to capacity with all sorts of technical equipment. After several sweaty and tiring hours of unloading, we had just one large crate left to unload—but wait. The union got wind of our activities, or so they had us believe. Out came seven or eight pot- bellied union workers hollering and threatening with their token petite, loudmouthed woman in tow. Their leader rudely informed our contact that the unloading of any truck’s haul into the hotel was strictly for union workers only. Our contact had no idea, and he meekly let everyone know. He was from another state, so he wasn’t expected to know the rules of each hotel in the entire US. The union leader made it known, within our earshot, that each union worker was to be paid in full (in excess of the hours they'd already worked or not) for each hour that we unloaded the truck. Our contact sent us home with regular pay as we were just about done anyway. There were several cameras on the loading dock. There's no way the union didn't know we were there. I'm pretty perceptive and read into the union workers' faces. I could tell that this was very well orchestrated and certainly no coincidence. I'm not saying that all unions are bad, but the poor things you do hear about them can be verified by me firsthand. I wonder how many times they pulled this stunt at this hotel and elsewhere. I know everything but can prove nothing.

More Fun than a Barrel of Monkeys

Various Dates, 1999–2000

've worked at this assignment many times over a one-year period in Malden, so I have some different but interesting memories that I'll share. This food company provided muffins, cake icing, and other dessert assortments type offerings for companies to buy and sell in the retail market. The boss noticed quickly that I was attentive to the company's every need. Another permanent worker broke the side of a machine while crashing a cart into it. The boss was informed of this. Later on I pieced together the broken parts to the best of my ability. I got a good enough feel for the dynamic at hand and could tell the boss figured it was me who fixed it, although he jokingly asked the employee if it was his doing. I guess he hadn't had any confidence in him. There were huge vats above the work area that usually contained pie filling or cake icing. All the ingredients were mixed up there for the final product. Down below, we had these plastic barrels that we would fill the customers' orders with—let's say cherry pie filling, as an example. Different-sized barrels needed loading, so we manually pulled the handle down until the product in the barrel reached the full line. I got proficient at the timing needed to ensure no overflow but, as I noticed, even the boss made mistakes. No matter how many years one did this, pushing the handle the wrong way on occasion was inevitable, resulting in scorching hot pie filling overflow. It was kind of comical to see the urgency to turn the handle the other way, not only because of product waste but also to see the quick moves to avoid third-degree burns. Once, while filling the barrels, I noticed there was a small amount of the machine's oil in the mix that I was told was miniscule and accepted by the customers. *Delicious*, I thought. If it was noticed, the standard practice was to use a large spoon to scoop it out. The same employee who crashed his cart into the machine earlier never used the spoon but instead stuck his finger in the batter directly—gross, isn't it? In fact, being a temp, I often asked him questions to get a better understanding of procedures. He was kind of mean and lashed out at me one time. I was just trying to get a better feel for a certain technique and asked, "Why does it go like this?" to which he shouted, "Because I said so, that's why!" *OK, enough said*, I thought. The muffins and other treats were great, though. Apparently, a mouse thought so, too. But unfortunately, he was trapped in the bottom of a trash bucket on one of those throwaway sticky papers.

He looked up and squeaked at me for help, but I was in the middle of the work area and people were watching. I'm so sorry, mouse, but at least I was able to redeem myself by helping many of your fellow rodents since then.

Epitome of a Witch?—Nah

March 29, 1999; September 25, 2001; September 28–
October 2, 2001

I worked on three occasions during a more than two-year period for a cosmetics company in Medford, and I did so in their small warehouse. The first time I showed up, however, I was taken aback by the appearance of the warehouse manager, who looked like a stereotypical witch. She had long, black straw-like hair, a crinkly face, and of course the wart on her nose. She was also a hard-ass, which only enhanced her witch image. I was half ready to receive a spell of some sort in certain instances. But in the end, I won her over with my warm smile and by exceeding her work expectations. We had laughs and jokes even, so it was a pleasant time, despite my first impression of her.

One Cheek or Tongue in Cheek?

November 12–14, 1999; November 18–19, 1999

I visited a large accounting firm twice for a few days, each in a one-week period in Boston. It almost had the two of us temps for an overnight stay in New York City to unload what we had just packed. It didn't work out, probably for various reasons—insurance, logistics, and so on. We packed plenty into the truck. We took apart several heavy and shoddily assembled meeting tables, chairs, and dry-erase boards. All were to be used by the company for a few days in New York City and returned for us to unload. The meeting tables that were oddly assembled were done by permanent employees who weren't there at the time, as I'd found out. Several pieces of the table had to be joined together at different angles to become one cohesive unit. Some pieces were jammed together with different screws, bolts, and washers. They were clearly hard to break down for shipping. Out of curiosity, I asked our contact, "In what manner was this put together?" He thought for a moment and said, "Half-assed." Based on his demeanor, I presumed he was embarrassed but maybe half joking?

Do You Want Some Popcorn?

December 10, 1999; December 30, 1999; February 28, 2000; March 15, 2000; May 30, 2000

I worked at an Internet start-up company five times over a several-month period in Cambridge. I remember feeling badly because one time I overheard something. An employee who might have been the hiring manager told his subordinate to "scrape the bottom of the barrel," referring to filling a position that maybe was hard to occupy. Those potential employees probably had no idea that this was the case for them. I hoped they were hired and more than met their potential and were highly regarded. Another time I was there, I was accompanied by another temp. I remember busting my butt and dripping with sweat while putting together shelving units and the like—only to be watched and not helped by the other temp. When I finally said something, he told me, "You were doing such a good job, and I didn't want to ruin it since you were on a roll." That may have been true, but as we went along I found out he was more lazy than helpful with the other projects we'd had. I definitely thought about offering him some refreshments. This was going to be a long movie, and he was getting comfortable.

February 4, 2000

S ince this one-day job was one of my first, it made my one and only defeat even more difficult. But the wind remained—and still remains—in my sails. The defeat I'm referring to was at a company in Boston that helps college students earn various shopping discounts with many business partners. I was confident as I did various duties throughout the day, until my contact opened the closet door to the next project. I was supposed to dispose of a metal pole attached to a huge slab of concrete. It looked like a street sign that had been ripped right out of the sidewalk by a backhoe. No one seemed to know why or how long it was in this closet. How convenient that I was the lucky one who was supposed to remove it. Well, I certainly tried. It was probably three to four hundred pounds. You couldn't really dead-lift it and carry it since the pole would hit the top of the doorway; it was too heavy anyway. I'm pretty strong and physically fit, but this was ridiculous! It was way too heavy to roll. Even if I could roll it, the flooring would be damaged due to not only the weight but also the jagged edges of the concrete. Even in the strongman competitions, the men wouldn't have to lift something heavy and then have to walk a far distance and down a flight of stairs. So I couldn't do it either. To be asked in the first place was ludicrous. Technically, I was defeated as I couldn't fulfill the customer's request. I still had my pride though, and I'm glad the customer never complained to my company about this incident. If they had, it probably would have made for a more humorous story. I want to know if it's still in that closet today, all these years later.

February 9, 2000

I had a one-day job in Boston working for a newspaper that had employed several temps. The project required the insertion of bricks into the base of a plastic newspaper holder to protect against tipping due to the wind and weather. Most of the temps sought out the easiest job of the day: unscrewing the lip of the base in order to insert the bricks and then screwing it back in afterward. As always I sought out the toughest job in a given assignment. In this case, it was bare-handing about a thousand bricks and tossing them into the bases of the units. Why they didn't provide gloves was a mystery; my hands were ripped apart and quite bloody from the repeated motions of jagged brick handling. When the screws were loosened, there wasn't much room for the bricks to fit through the plastic lid. It took some finagling and more bloodshed to squeeze them in. I also did the second toughest job of the day in this remote, freezing warehouse with no supplies or refreshments to refuel us. (Thankfully, the customer went out and got us cokes and pretzels.) I had to unbox the plastic newspaper holders in the first place. The cardboard boxes that contained the holders were so thick, they couldn't be cut using the measly razor blades we were given. Instead, we had to rip off the top and pull the entire heavy box straight over the four-foot holder in order to clear it. Brutal core strength was needed each of the hundreds of times it was done. At the end of the day, my hands looked like they were rotting off from all the cuts and scrapes from the cardboard boxes, razor blades, and especially the bricks. A fun day, though I'm glad it was only one.

Two Cheeks

February 22–25, 2000; December 13–19, 2000

I worked at the warehouse of a comic-book store on two occasions in a span of less than a year in Brighton. A lot of interesting, comical, and quirky people worked here as permanent employees, as one might expect from a comic-book distributor. And there were plenty of different responsibilities and duties to be had here by me. One time I was working on a skid of heavy boxes. I was soaked with sweat, so my clothes clung to me like flies on...so it was no surprise what happened next: *rrriipp!*—right down the back of my pants. Good thing it was near the end of the day, and no one really noticed. I escaped without embarrassment. It helped that the employees probably had a sense of humor, as I mentioned before. I can imagine the relentless, unmerciful jokes that would have come my way—especially as a temp. We're not always looked at favorably.

It's Just a Free T-Shirt, OK?

April 4, 2000; October 3, 2001

I worked twice in the period of about a year and a half for a production company that put together various trade shows or expositions in Boston. One time a fellow temp practically demanded a similar T-shirt that our contact's staff had on. It was painful to witness. What made it sillier is that the shirt had a ridiculous-looking multicolored cartoon *Tyrannosaurus -rex* on it. The company was from California, and one of our contacts said he would have some shipped to us. I was standing right there as he asked if anyone else would like one. I didn't want to insult him, so I told him OK. He happened to jot down my address, and suddenly it was my responsibility in the coming weeks to find out which temps wanted them and where they were. Darn that woman for begging for the T-shirt! The shirts never came, and I forgot about it. Then, my company called inquiring about them since the woman called complaining about me. So here I am, in charge of some dumb shirts that should never have been requested in the first place. I'm sure it made me look bad in front of some of the office staff that didn't know me. Later, that same woman complained about me again. It was pretty soon after the T-shirt incident during a quick customer service-type job that she was loafing on. She was painting her nails and just watching me explain things to customers. Then she called our company and said I wasn't explaining things properly to the customers. This was outrageous to me; I take great pride and make sure I do all jobs more than properly. I never saw her again. I hope my company cut ties with her. My reputation is as good as gold with my company, so they likely never bought into any of the slander against me and maybe even other temps. Good riddance, Mrs. T-Shirt.

April 6, 2000; December 12, 2000; January 1, 2001;
October 12, 2001; February 20–22, 2002

I visited a financial firm five times in an almost two-year period in Boston. My contact there was very nice. She would be glad to see me each time. "Oh, Speedy Gonzales is here," she'd say. She was referring to the speed at which I stuffed envelopes for her, which was always my job there. The number of paper inserts that needed to be stuffed varied. One particular project called for between seven and ten bonded papers to be folded into threes, which is very thick and difficult to do, especially when it's all day long. After that they were inserted into envelopes. After a while, my fingers wore down from the strength it took to bear down and fold that amount. And then it happened—a paper cut practically to the bone—*ouch!* The papers were reprinted due to the blood, and my contact helped me take care of the wound. Surprisingly, I didn't need stitches, even though the cut was deep. It did finally stop bleeding, and Speedy Gonzalez was at it again with a nice, new battle scar to boot!

May 8–11, 2000; March 4–5, 2002

I visited this bank twice in an almost two-year period in Boston. My most memorable duty was
helping them move into their new corporate offices
downtown. There were dozens upon dozens of very
heavy paper boxes. Some held brand-new paper for
the copiers and fax machines, and others contained
corporate paperwork or binders that were equally as
heavy. They had to be loaded methodically into an
oversized closet. This closet was pretty far away from
the boxes, so I tried to minimize the trips by putting
the maximum number of boxes on the carts that were
provided. To say the carts were heavy when loaded
is an understatement. Just to get the carts rolling, I
needed every ounce of strength. The same could be
said to keep them moving. My sweat flew everywhere.
I felt like Conan the Barbarian as I thought about a
scene in the movie where he had to push this heavy
grain wheel around and around. He started as a boy in
slavery, but years of pushing this wheel transformed

him into Arnold Schwarzenegger. Great workout, and I made short time of the project, too.

Side Note:

WITHOUT THE POSSIBILITY OF PAROLE?

I had a passing conversation with an employee who had been at this bank for twenty-five years already. She told me that she could never do what I did as far as doing different jobs all the time. Without being too harsh about it, I told her I could never do what she did either—a prison sentence of twenty-five years to life. Well, at least we were honest with each other.

Side Note:

ANGER AND OUTRAGE ON MY PART

In my brief time working at the bank, I'd met the president, CEO, and COO. I worked right in their area most of the time. They liked my work and as a parting gift gave me a few sweatshirts with their bank logo. Soon after, I decided to open an account at one of their branches as I liked their business model. The branch manager happened to be the one who opened my account and was surprised when I took off my jacket and had on one of their sweatshirts. She said those were for employees only and asked where I got it. I told her that I worked there briefly and with some top executives who gave me the shirts. She asked who, so I named them. All true. She seemed suspicious for some reason but did open the account for me. When I got home, there was a message from the bank's security on my machine demanding that I call them back ASAP. When I called, they tore into me, demanding to know the nature of my contact with the executives, where I got the sweatshirt, and why I wanted the account opened. When I mentioned the word sweatshirts (plural), a new sense of shock was now in place. "How many do you have?" they asked, as they yelled at me, demanding the return of the sweatshirts. They said my account with them was now closed; further, if I came within one hundred feet of any of their bank branches, I'd be hit with a restraining order. *What the heck is going on here?* I wondered. I wasn't sure why this was happening to me, but I wanted an end to it. Not wanting to risk legal action, I returned the two sweatshirts to a local branch and never heard from them again. I was angry that I was treated that way and barely had the chance to defend myself or tell my story. To make matters worse, under duress I told them what company I worked for and, of course, was called by them. Once I explained what had happened, my company didn't seem too concerned. Doesn't their call to my company confirm my story anyway? That I'd worked at the bank on certain dates and had come into contact with certain people? To this day, this whole mess is still a mystery to me. Since I was given a few sweatshirts and worked briefly with some top executives, I'm public enemy number one?

A Game of Frisbee with State Troopers Anybody?

August 10–September 21, 2000; October 16–November 3, 2000

I worked for an automatic toll-collecting company on two occasions and in two different cities, East Boston and Chelsea. Local residents got toll discounts on the area highways, bridges, and tunnels. With the current system, people could hand tickets to the toll takers for the discount. But the new system launched during my assignment had transponders attached to the inside of the automobile's windshield, hidden from the driver's view, behind the rearview mirror. Every time someone passed by a toll, the discounted amount would be automatically deducted from the person's credit/debit card or bank account. The goal was to alleviate bottlenecking.

On designated dates the residents were notified to come to a location to get these free transponders since, as of a certain date, the tickets would no longer be valid. For years they'd used the tickets system, and it was smooth sailing. As a result, most were upset with the change. There were several temps whose jobs were to hand out the transponders, process the paperwork for the residents, and explain in full detail just what the heck was going on. Resistance to change is commonplace, and there was no exception this time. Many people yelled and cursed at me. One older man in particular comes to mind. He bent over and hollered mercilessly at me and reasoned that I'd never experienced the death of a wife, so he didn't expect me to understand his frustration. Although this was true, how could he have known that I hadn't experienced it, since he never asked? I still don't think that's a reason to berate me drill-sergeant style. What did this have to do with my explaining the program to him? In any case, there were some who were thrilled with the new program, so that was a good thing.

Since there were hundreds of people who came in droves on the designated dates, state troopers were deployed. There were lulls, too. Some of the giveaways included Frisbees, so before long we were playing Frisbee with the state troopers. They were great with behind-the-back catches, between-the-legs grabs, and the like. They were in full uniform too, which made it all the more fun. This was seemingly an odd pairing, and I wondered what passersby thought! It was good to break the stress for all involved, especially the residents. One day, I got a ride home from a state trooper, and as we pulled up I realized I was locked in the backseat. To let me out, he had to open the door from the outside. I guess it was a good thing that I was surprised since having experience in such matters is distasteful. I lived just around the corner, but it was cold so I jogged home. Afterward, I wondered how it looked—me getting out of a state police car and then running from a state trooper? Just another humorous turn in the life of a temp.

Side Note:

STRIPTEASE

One of our contacts worked for the toll-collecting company itself. She was an attractive young female who often flirted with me. She even went as far as flashing me; sometimes she lifted her shirt and other times quickly pulled her pants down for me when no one was around. Geez, I didn't know I was that irresistible. Her behavior was obviously totally unprofessional, if not illegal, but she was our client. I was stuck in a predicament, to say the least. Soon after this display, my fellow temp confided in me that the same lady had directed some racial comments toward her. I decided to tell her what the lady did to me. Two strikes and she was out, in our book. We decided to go to our company and tell what had happened to each of us. It turned out that she was working for our company the whole time but from a different office. She was soon to be hired by the toll-collecting company. On a professional level, she probably wanted to be perceived as a person of power and not just another temp. She was fired that day and never to be heard from again. I wonder if some other temps that we worked with on that job had any stories to share of their own. No one mentioned her again after she got canned, though.

Tiptoe through the...Envelopes

October 5, 2000; November 19, 2001; February 11, 2002

I worked at a college in Boston three times in just over two years. Mostly I stuffed envelopes. Envelope stuffing runs the gamut. Sometimes I'd put generic pieces of paper into generic envelopes; other times I had to match up names on the inserts to the envelopes. The latter was the case on this day. The problem was that my contact had printed out the inserts and envelopes in such a way that there was no order. I don't know if it was feasible for her to print them in alphabetical order and she just didn't. Or, for whatever reason, maybe she just couldn't. Regardless, they were in disarray. The fastest way to pair up the insert to the envelope was to lay them out, first on the table, then on some chairs, and then on the floor. I ended up using almost the whole floor of the conference room. *OK, I have a Zach Taylor envelope; just let me find his insert. All right, two steps to the left and around a chair. Careful, just don't step on any papers—OK, I found it. Next, a Stephanie Maximus insert. And so on.* It was really a lot of fun, and I did manage to match them all up by the deadline. I think I perfected certain dance moves that I didn't know I had.

Terrorist-Funding Company?

October 9, 2000

worked for only one day at a technology company in Boston. As of this writing, there are indictments against the former CEO and CFO alleging that they had financial connections with a terrorist organization. It's scary to look back and think what might have been going on behind closed doors.

The Jury's Out...on Me, Though

December 12, 2000

About twenty-five to thirty of us temps were sent out one day to a lawyer's office for a mock jury. This was one of those ultracrammed mock trials squeezed into one day. The hope was that a fair and accurate decision would come by the end of the day, ideally the same outcome that would result from a real multiday trial. But of course the goal was to avoid a real trial and settle out of court to save both time and money for all parties concerned. When it was time to deliberate, we gathered in a room. It was decided that I'd be the foreperson based on my interest, enthusiasm, and good understanding of what needed to be accomplished. Sometimes the reality of real trial jurors is that they just want to go home as soon as possible and thus lose the passion or patience required to make a fair decision. Well, in this case, it was magnified tenfold. We had tons of information to sift through with limited time, and I wanted to be thorough. In reality, the outcome was going to affect all parties, but I got the feeling that most of the jurors didn't take it seriously because it was only a mock jury. As I tried to placate the jurors, whose frustration was mounting, I realized something was missing—a gavel, which is exactly the tool I needed to control this anxious group. Negative comments were sometimes laced with profanity as the group just wanted to leave. The line-item questions to be determined were hastily decided and then—like monkey see, monkey do—just copied by other jurors in an effort to end it quickly to appease me and the lawyers. While some empathized with me, the frustrated mob won out. In a regular trial, this would never be allowed. In the end, I wondered if this helped or hurt the parties involved. I hoped there were several mock juries being held specifically for them to balance it out a bit. I've been on other mock juries as well with fewer people and a lot more time to decide people's fates. It seems this one was poorly orchestrated from the beginning, but I tried my best as the foreperson should.

Complimentary Breakfast

January 16–18, 2001

This three-day job was at a public television station in Brighton, so I was especially happy to help. I've always been supportive of people directly contributing to TV, radio, and Internet programming. My task was to set up specific shelving and storage units in one of their maintenance areas. The work was heavy yet needed very detailed measurements. Immediately I jumped headfirst into the work. My contact was taken aback. While eating his morning muffin, he commented that he's never seen a temp work with such enthusiasm and that they're usually lackadaisical in their approach. Unfortunately, temps do not often receive praise. I was proud of this compliment and hoped I gave temps, in general, a better reputation. And maybe, just maybe, he'd spread the word about his positive encounter with a temp. That's one small step for temps.

January 23–June 30, 2001

This job, which lasted about half a year, was certainly an interesting ride. A company that produces tape, sticky notes, and other products hired us to work in Boston's public libraries. One job was to put security strips into every book. The strip was sticky on both sides and very thin like a flattened straw with about the same width and length. The goal was to open a book to a random page and insert the strip deep into the crease. When you closed the book, both sides of the strips adhered to the pages, making it virtually invisible. The interior of the strip contained a metal of some sort. The security barriers were eventually erected near the exit of the library, and an alarm would go off if someone tried to steal a book. When a person borrowed a book, the staff deactivated the strip electronically—and activated it when returned. Some books that were longer than the strip didn't present a problem since all that mattered was the strip inside it. But many books were shorter than the strip, so we had to do some cutting along the way that would impede our progress. It was a nice system as we had custom-made rolling carts with the strip-dispensing machine in the center and wings on either side that collapsed. An ergonomic paddle that was dropped right into the slot in the machine automatically inserted a strip onto it. So we'd take it out, slap it in the center of the book, and repeat. The moment the machine inserted the strip onto the paddle was pretty loud, though; it sounded like a dull thud. A library's acoustics aren't the greatest for any type of noise, so inevitably people complained.

We started out on a few small branches of the library, probably to familiarize ourselves with the process before going to the main branch. I was put in charge of everything once we got there. We started out with about six people, and at my discretion we would add more temps. The project was supposed to last no more than three years. Millions of books had to be done and with only six of us. We started strategically, row by row. Books on shelves are never in perfect order, but our task was to keep them in the order we found them. People would come and take books off the shelf while we were working, of course, but the fail-safe was that in the coming weeks the staff had their own machines. The staff could check whether a book that would be returned to the shelf had a strip in it. As we got into a groove, I added more and more temps. It was a calculated trade-off; more noise ultimately meant less time overall that we'd be disturbing the public. There were too many variables with contracts between my company, the tape company, and the library; there was never any clear indicator to me if the contract should go shorter or longer. I decided to finish it sooner rather than later by adding even more temps.

We had a reasonable minimum number of books that needed to be done hourly. I tested out the process several times to make sure it was fair and did more than twice the minimum every time. That made me confident about the minimum that was being asked of the temps. I had to let some of them go here and there for many reasons, including laziness, talking too much, no-shows, and sleeping. Some temps even sat on the floor curled up with a good book, as if they were at home. I was very patient, but they sank themselves ultimately as I talked with each temp about my observations and let them know the deal beforehand. It's funny just how many temps came up to me over the course of the project just wanting to share some of the interesting reads they'd found.

From six it swelled to around fifty temps as we conquered those aisles. My company had an agreement with a halfway house to employ some ex-cons.

They asked me if it was OK to send some, and I agreed since I don't discriminate. What did I get myself into? Some interesting characters emerged from this bunch. I didn't ask, but it was inevitable that some would tell me their stories or share how much time was left for them in the halfway house. Some had the stereotypical rough look of an ex con, while others looked normal. Upon arrival every single day at work, one person from the group was to call his or her base and report the names of the people who showed up, ensuring everyone was accounted for. They all gelled together pretty well with the other temps but were overfriendly with the females, as expected; being cooped up for any time might have that effect. But I kept my eye on them and the others, and all was well. A guy named Ron had bolted but was caught and put back behind bars. With so many temps, the atmosphere over the months became very friendly, family-like almost, especially when we finished the public areas and worked in the private buildings that housed gazillions of more books with very few library employees around. A happy worker is a good worker, so I gave them more freedom in these private buildings, which were holding areas for many book titles. I let them express themselves more loudly and joke around, but nothing too drastic as the job had to be done and I didn't want to offend anyone. I remember a particular area of one floor that was uniquely designed. Around one corner, the aisles of bookshelves had the appearance of being infinite, sort of like looking at two mirrors at a certain angle. It was a super long hallway—breathtaking. I'd bring certain temps to the area without explaining why. "Turn around," I'd say. Their responses ranged from gasps to "What the hell?" to "We're never going to finish." This was close to the end of the project, so people thought we were cruising until they saw it. It seemed insurmountable. Not that we really had a deadline, but it's natural to want to finish something once started. Of course, some temps needed that job for as long as possible and preferred a much smaller staff to extend the work over three years.

We did finally finish the main branch. Next, we had to cover the twenty some odd branches around Boston. For this project, the staff had to be reduced to around six again, since the branches were pretty small compared to the main branch. It was tough to choose who was coming with me since we all had become pretty close over the months. Some volunteered to depart for various reasons, but unfortunately the remaining temps just had to be cut. We used a rental truck to haul the machines branch to branch. Fortunately, one temp was a former cabbie and knew the city well, which clinched his spot. He was only an OK worker and would have been cut otherwise. We would arrange to meet at a certain place on a given day, depending on the branch location. He would navigate me daily, so it worked out well. He was one of the ex-cons who called himself "the Chief" since he was related to the chief of the Nigerian village he came from. The Chief was quite an arrogant character, bragging about the financial crimes he'd committed, saying, "They got what they deserved." He'd mumble random details here and there and allude to some of the more sinister activities in which he partook. Still, the Chief was our source of amusement back when we were at the main branch. A group of us was at lunch in the cafeteria one day when in walks the Chief. He'd come from the restroom with a line of toilet paper that he'd inadvertently tucked in the back of his pants. The line extended all the way through the cafeteria, across the hallway, and to the men's room—easily fifty feet! The crowd roared with laughter and jeers. The look on his face was definitely priceless. It's hard to believe that it stretched that far, but it was nearly a straight shot. My final story involving the Chief isn't a pleasant one, though. We arranged to meet at a train station near the end of the project so he could navigate me as usual. I waited forty-five minutes extra, and he was still a no-show. I had to go as the others were waiting for me. He did finally show up at work. He was upset with me even though he was the one late to the station. After complaining to me at length, he said,

"If I had a gun I'd shoot you." I was dumbfounded and disappointed since we did build camaraderie in our time together. I was upset but didn't show it. As there were only a few days left, I decided to say nothing to anyone about it. I suppose he could have gotten into real trouble considering his parole situation. After taking everything into account, I decided that he'd had enough trouble already, and I wanted to end the project on a good note.

I do have other memories from these branches that are worth mentioning. One of the branches was infested with crawling centipedes, which bothered many temps as there were many stacks of books to be handled. One of the girls dropped a book that fell under a desk. Well, here was my chance. As she crawled under the desk to retrieve it, I lightly yelled, "Centipede!" to which she let out a hellacious scream. She was going to kill me after that, but it was worth it. Just another day at a quiet library.

We came across more than one cockroach along the way, too. Unlike the centipedes, though, they were actually interested in the books—not to read but to consume the glue and maybe some of the pages. These huge cockroaches had an almost never-ending supply of food in a nice, quiet, and warm environment. I might even be tempted.

I was given the keys to a particular branch since the main librarian resented our being there at all. His goal was to have us there several hours before the branch would open and then for just a few hours after that. Although it was pretty early for most of us, I agreed, which put him at ease and made everyone involved happy. We arrived the first day, and as we were just getting settled in, something surprising happened. Two police officers showed up. It turns out that we tripped a silent alarm. Thanks for the warning, Mr. Librarian. I could only imagine what it looked like to the officers. Six or seven people—some of whom were ex-cons (and looked it)—were shocked to see the police. They asked me for my ID, and of course I had only a state-issued one and no library ID. It was the machines that we were using and my explanation that saved us in the end. It was so early in the morning that we couldn't have contacted an authorized person, like my contact or the librarian. I'm not sure how the police would have proceeded otherwise. Did the librarian forget to tell us about the alarm? I guess we'll never know.

One more task needed to be completed after the branches were done. Three of us were to head to Norwood, Massachusetts, to finish a private building chock-full of books, but it never materialized. We were taken off the project in favor of the library workers. Later I found out that when we worked in the private buildings, library staff complained that we littered the place with soda cans, bottles, and snack wrappers. It wasn't true. In my initial inspection, I noticed the place was already littered, and some of the cans were relics from the eighties or before. To ensure we wouldn't add to the mess, I was on top of it daily. In fact, we improved it. While picking up books, we came into contact with some trash, so we just tossed it. I'm not saying we were perfect but simply good at what we did. We were probably the only contractor that had worked in those private buildings in decades. Otherwise, it had to be the library employees. It was easy for them to point the finger, those same employees who complained and made us look bad. The few of us who were left were disgusted by this allegation and ended the project with a grunt. As a temp, one encounters more different layers of red tape than does a permanent employee. The representative whom we worked for knew that it wasn't our fault but had to balance the many entities that she had to please. I'm glad she understood at least, and I harbor no hard feelings toward her. I'm also glad that the Boston public libraries have less theft, thanks in small part to us temps.

August 30–September 4, 2001

This approximately one-week job is the measuring stick by which all of my past and future temp jobs will be measured. I've performed hundreds of physically challenging jobs over the years, but this one far surpasses them all. Often, when you get the call for a job, the description doesn't match the job. It's understandable, though, as customers' needs do change. I was told I'd be rearranging some desks at a school for one day. Instead, I got an epic week from hell. This school was a pre-k through eighth-grade private school way in the sticks, Manchester specifically. It was summer, the best time to tackle special projects and complete minor construction. The order of events is not important here, so I'll just tell them at random. Although there were many tasks I did there over the week, I'll mention some of the more interesting ones. Every day, it seemed, had its own theme.

METAL THEME:

On my first day, it was pouring out. A huge pile of metal beams or poles was lying on the ground; the school must have disassembled a structure of some sort. The backhoe was near, so it must have done its job by placing the heap there. With little help, I stacked random pieces of metal into certain piles. They were very heavy, sharp, and slippery from the rain. The work gloves I'd been given were shredded after just a few minutes of work. Then it was my hands that got shredded—just my hands, though. No big deal, right? I'm not used to being that far from the city and saw some interesting-looking salamanders and huge spiders, too, as I organized the pile. There were also some field mice that we disturbed. One ran close to my contact, so he booted him into the sky. It looked pretty funny, but I do love animals and am against any sort of cruelty.

WOOD THEME:
A longer-term project was to complete an outdoor-ropes course with both high and low elements. In order to accomplish this, we laid down the groundwork by cutting down certain trees. We'd used a chainsaw, and that was probably the only easy task during my tenure there. It would have taken forever with an ax, to be sure. After we cut the trees down, we chopped them into pieces about three feet long. Well, yours truly had to squat and lift every single chunk of wood and then transport it across the forest to a designated area. The narrow part of the trees wasn't a problem, as I gathered many pieces together, but some of the

thick trunks were a different story. They were bulky and extraordinarily heavy. We did find a bees' nest. My contact aimed the bee spray right into the belly of the nest, and then we took off, which helped us blow off some steam. We had some laughs, and all was well.

ROCK THEME:

There was to be some paving up a rocky, dirty incline between buildings. In the meantime, the larger rocks needed to be removed to make it easier for the paving. Certain machinery couldn't navigate the incline, or else I assume it would have been used. As I worked, some of the large rocks turned into boulders as I unearthed them with my bare hands. Just like the wood chunks, these boulders had to be carried to a particular area. Each time I walked back to get the next boulder, I could see the backhoe, which seemed to be smiling at me. I felt like Atlas when he was holding up the world on his shoulders. I have no idea what some of them weighed, but I just smile when I think about it. I found areas to hold on to, though, since each boulder was uniquely shaped. Years later, I found out that there are actual contests with men carrying boulders while walking far distances, which is exactly what I did. Except I did it for hours and not just mere minutes! Maybe I should enter the contest.

INSECT THEME:

I had to enter the attic of a house that was on the property of the school. It would eventually be made into a regular room for one of the staff. My job was to strip a particular layer of wood from the entire room. The nails were as old and rusty as could be. I was given some goggles, a hammer, a nail remover, a pry bar, and a ladder. I had to ask for some ear-protection head-phones, since the high pitch of the hammer on the nail remover left my ear in excruciating pain. It didn't help that it was over a hundred degrees and very humid (where's the rain now?). The place was also crawling with insects of all sorts, but mostly carpenter ants. Some people use the phrase "it's like pulling teeth," but I now say "it's like pulling nails," since each nail was rusty and stuck like heck to the wood. It was a challenge to dislodge each nail, and I'm pretty strong, so that wasn't the issue. On top of that was the natural angle of the inside of the roof. I had to sit on the ladder at uncomfortable angles to get the job done as I worked my way down. Once I got to the floor level, I had to roll my way into the corner and stretch out my hands to get at the nails. I was responsible for many crushed ant carcasses as I inched my way down the entire flooring section. I drank the little bit of water I had right away, and I had several more hours to go. But I was determined to get out of there.

HOLE THEME:

Many of us have dug holes in our lives, right? I have dug some holes as well, but one hole was sheer torture. I think it was for a new post, but only one hole needed to be dug. It needed to be several feet deep with a wide circumference. There were trees all around, and thus ten thousand roots got in my way as I dug. At my disposal was an old, crappy shovel and an equally junky hoe. It took me hours of hard labor (mostly in the sun) for one lousy hole. All I could think about were the trees, which didn't shade me. It was probably revenge for my repeated stabbing and cutting at them.

The whole experience was similar to the TV show *Survivor*: the last person standing won. Almost every day a new temp was sent to help me, but each quickly disappeared. I wonder what my company's office thought. For some reason I'd stayed, while the others bailed. I would have done this for free and was totally up for any challenge thrown at me.

The assignment ended as the school year was about to begin; regular duties were in place for the permanent employees. The duties they'd left for the temps had been predetermined, it seemed. When I got home each day, the first thing I did was throw out my clothes. They were ripped to shreds and had rust, mud, and ant guts all over them—and who knows what else. I long for another temp challenge such as this one but have yet to find one.

Side Note:

NICE GUY BUT...

One of the janitors there assisted me on some of the smaller projects. We ended up talking on breaks, and he confided in me that he had been fired at his previous job. It was at another school where he was let go for having lunch in the cafeteria with a young girl. I wondered if his current job knew the circumstances behind his firing and, if so, why he was still hired.

Side Note:

SLAM DUNK

I was quite surprised one day while working in the gymnasium. I noticed the basketball backboards and rims were very low. I assumed it was because it was an elementary school, and the kids wouldn't be able to heave the ball up to a regular-sized hoop. I've never been able to dunk on a regular-sized rim, always falling just short. When I was a kid, my friends and I would sometimes lay down shopping carts or trash barrels to use as springboards for dunking. It was fun, but here was my first opportunity to do it from the ground. I grabbed a basketball and made a leaping slam dunk with a scream that could be heard for miles, with all of the echoes that a gym holds. It was quite exhilarating for me, as I've always wanted to do it. I was working with another temp that day, and we had lots of fun for a few minutes on our break. We tried to top each other with creative and stylistic dunks. It was a much-needed respite from the backbreaking work of the day.

September 10–12, 2001

This three-day job at a printing company in Malden had two of us temps walking in circles clockwise around a large rectangular table. The goal was to pick up, in order, large, beautifully designed cards that were printed out to form the complete collection for a given customer's showcase. It was sort of like a brochure in card form. I was trying to use the utmost speed and accuracy as I always do on jobs, much to the chagrin of my fellow temp. He let me know in no uncertain terms that he was going to take his sweet time, so we worked it out that I would fly by him rotation after rotation, but in a respectful way. It was definitely a comical scene with the two of us marching around at two very different speeds!

Side Note:

9/11

The middle day of this three-day job was 9/11. There was an employee there who seemed crazy because she would just walk around saying peculiar things all the time. On that day she said a plane had crashed into a building. I noticed some of the employees going to a break room to see the TV. Then the boss told everyone to go home. *What's going on here?* I'd discounted what she said based on her previous weird comments—until I got home and saw the news.

September 14, 2001

worked at a law firm for one day in Boston, which was only three days after 9/11. Upon my arrival at the outside gate of the building, I was met by a state police officer. He asked for my ID, and I explained that I didn't have any, as I was a temporary worker for the day. He shouted at me and demanded an ID. I then realized he meant a state-issued ID and not a work ID. We realized that we were both at fault and were just trying to feel our way in a new world. After I showed him my ID, we talked briefly about how we were on the same side but just cautious about a lot of new things now.

Call Girl

October 19, 2001; November 1, 2001; April 8–12, 2002

I worked several times at many different photography companies, mostly at sessions for college students' senior pictures. We temps would travel to the campuses and set up the equipment. One time, as I was registering a student, he made me a proposition. He offered me a young Vietnamese beauty for the night. He said one call was all he needed to make, and I could meet her when I was ready. It was odd timing, since I was signing him up for a photo, but I guess he grabbed every opportunity he had to make money. I told him that I was all set. He might have really needed the money, as he persisted in trying to get me to bite, just out of earshot of the photographer. In fact, the photographer did hear something and thought I was the pimp somehow. He glared at me and let me know in private that this was an inappropriate conversation. He knew he had to be careful with his words, as there were way too many students who could have easily overheard our conversation. At the end of the night, we talked about it to clear up any misunderstandings and even had a laugh, too. Man, the situations I find myself in.

Peanut Allergies—Maybe Not

November 5, 2001

This was to be a longer-term assignment at a peanut-butter factory in Everett. I was to work in their office to process orders and other paperwork. As soon as I arrived in the office, I could smell the peanuts. The office also had a lot of water damage, so it smelled of mildew. I was to temporarily take the place of an employee who was out due to cancer treatments. The desk was all grimy, and other foul chemical odors pervaded the air. I became worried that this whole situation was somehow related to the person's cancer, so I looked for a way out. There were people around, so I had to tell a white lie. I certainly didn't want to offend anyone by complaining about their working conditions. I called the representative from my company who sent me there, and I told him that I was allergic to peanuts and that the smell was bothering me. He pointed out that about a week earlier, when I helped him move, I was eating Reese's Peanut Butter Cups. I blurted out that it was just candy and not real peanut butter. He knew I was fibbing to get out of an unpleasant and depressing situation. He did me a favor, though, as I'd helped him out on numerous occasions. This was the first and only time that I ducked out of an assignment; usually, I look forward to new and exciting gigs. I guess I was overly concerned about chemical exposure at the time since my grandmother was battling cancer. I hope that employee did conquer her cancer and come back to work all the better for it. I'm used to brutal work, so this would've been an easy sit-down job; nonetheless, I was glad to be removed. Jelly anyone?

The President Was Frowned Upon by Many

November 29, 2001

For a few hours one morning, I had to hand out free copies of a money magazine at one of Boston's "T" train stops. The boss at my company's branch accompanied me, which was pretty rare. On the cover of the magazine was George W. Bush, who at the time was president. A lot of people sneered at me once they saw who was on the cover and refused the handout. I remember that his popularity was down at that time. Still, it was only a few months after 9/11, so one would think we'd be as united as ever. But deep-seated feelings are just that.

Paying Homage to My Late Friend

March 7–12, 2002

On this several-day job, I met up with a friend who had worked for me at the Boston Public Library assignment. I hadn't seen him for a while and didn't know he was going to work with me this go-around. I arrived before him on the first day. When the elevator doors opened and he saw me, he said, "What are you doing here? I thought you'd be a millionaire by now." We resumed our joking and camaraderie from that instant. We worked hard and laughed a lot over the next several days. On the last day, we didn't have much work to do. Our contact told us that as soon as we finished certain projects, we could go home with pay for the whole day. I worked quickly and methodically as usual, so we ended up going home very early. We said our good-byes and "see you next time around." The next day, I got a call from my company's office letting me know that he was killed the previous night. I couldn't believe it. A woman with only a driver's learning permit jumped the curb with her car and hit and killed him instantly. She then took off on foot but was caught. I won't get into the legal outcome regarding her, but somehow I felt guilty. What if I'd worked more slowly the previous day or talked with him more after work? I'm not blaming myself, but I think I was inadvertently responsible. I doubt he would have been in that exact spot if we had left work an hour later. We'll never know, but I won't forget my precious time and the great memories with my friend Charles Crockett. RIP. I bring a little piece of our fond memories together to every temp job.

March 13, 2002

ere was a one-day job that had two of us temps working for a company that translates books into many languages for publishers in Boston. It mostly entailed carrying the company's furniture and other miscellaneous items down to their storage unit in the basement. It was a dark, dank area in an otherwise nice office building. To avoid the hundreds of nails that were protruding through the ceiling above us, we crouched down, crablike, to carry the furniture and boxes. We made many trips, and since I was the taller of the two, I inevitably hit some of the rusty old nails—just a few minor scrapes on my cranium. When we finished it felt great to walk upright again. Walking is one of life's simple pleasures.

I Told You So

June 3–11, 2002

Many of us temps were sent to help open up a new bookstore in an exclusive Boston mall. There were tons of random jobs to be done. The duties ranged from unpacking boxes to pricing CDs to unloading pallets of boxes and books. I tore up the place as always and was offered a permanent job by the manager. I told him I was just there for the week that we were requested—and for the workout. A few days later, the manager was observing my work unbeknown to me. He told me that he saw what I meant, referring to my workout comment. I was doing double time while squatting down to place the books on the lower shelves. And quickly up again for more. I was offered a permanent position yet again, but again I respectfully declined. Bring on the next assignment, please.

Soaked in Sweat without Doing Gymnastics

June 28–30, 2002

For this three-day job, we temps were needed to move the small gymnastics company across the street to their new location in Cambridge. It was an out-of-the-way location, so traffic really wasn't an issue. I envisioned moving a trampoline and suddenly cars bouncing off it high into the air with the greatest of ease. We were joined by the gym staff and a lot of young female gymnasts. The girls were strong, but some of the mats were easily a few hundred pounds. There were so many items that needed to be transported, from huge mats to jump ropes. The large mats weren't only heavy but also long and wide. We needed several people around the perimeter to avoid dragging it on the ground. During the initial lift and throughout the walk, the smell of soaked sweat in the center and mildew on the bottom of the mat was almost enough to knock us out in true Olympic style! It was boiling hot out, so the staff used a key for the juice machine for free drinks for the duration. We rejoiced at the end of the last day since everything was brought over. The setting up of everything would be at the company's leisure. We tried out some equipment, rolling around a bit on some different mats. It was a nice release and fun to try out something new, the perfect springboard to whatever adventure came next.

The TSA Started Out with a Bang...a Humorous One, Though

June 30–October 18, 2002

There are plenty of good stories to share from my almost four-month job at the TSA. I was the only temp from my company, but there were dozens from our rival company. I'm not sure how that happened, though I did inquire. It was the inception of the TSA, and as such created many challenges. We took over a wing of Boston's Logan Airport Hilton Hotel for the duration. We set up shop to interview prospective TSA workers, which involved a number of steps. The hired employees would have at least some of their orientation there as well. It was pretty chaotic; every couple of days, different staff members flew in from all parts of the country. None of us really knew where they stood for sure. As a group, we did the best that we could, even though the reporting structure changed so often. After a while, it finally became better organized. I was the chief test proctor for potential new hires. We had two ridiculous tests to administer that I hope have been discontinued or at least improved.

THE SUITCASE-TEST SCENARIO #1:

We put four suitcases flat down on the floor. Each was in a rectangular holding area marked off with electrical tape and a corresponding number. They were laid down next to each other in the areas marked 1–4: suitcase #1 heavy, #2 lighter, #3 lightest, and #4 heaviest. The suitcase weight variations were kept from the applicants. They had to navigate around orange cones with the suitcases and then put the suitcases onto a table, which also had taped on it numbers 1–4. For this timed test, it didn't matter how quickly they finished but only that it was under the allotted time. Before the test, I had to recite a speech verbatim. It was fairly obvious what needed to be done for the test, but I wasn't allowed to reveal anything other than what I'd already mentioned. Their task was to follow the directions as I stated them. Although they were suitcases, we were supposed to call them boxes. My intervals of speech varied depending on how fast someone walked. Running wasn't permitted. OK, box one…around the cone…space one on the table…box two…around the cone…space two on the table, and so on until all four were on the table. The process was reversed after that, so they'd finish where they started, with all four suitcases on the floor in their respective areas. I said these words verbatim, according to the rules, each time. Every applicant had his or her own unique approach to this Olympics-style challenge. Some even took off their shoes to maximize speed. Others wore high heels and even at my urging wouldn't take them off. A few people grabbed the first box and sprinted, even though I told them only walking was permitted. They were given second chances as nerves were an issue for most. Others walked ridiculously slowly, knowing they were supposed to walk at a good clip since that was the point of the test. They failed, even though I encouraged them to pick up the pace. This test was fair regarding the required walking speed. As the first three boxes got progressively lighter, many figured out that the last would be the heaviest, so they prepared themselves accordingly. But not everyone guessed it. Some thought it would be the lightest, which brought me the most laughs (only on the inside, of course). Even if it had been the lightest, they should've still picked it up properly. Instead, they were grabbing it quickly with great momentum. One woman looked as if a lightning bolt had hit her as she grabbed that last box, and not just because she was shocked at the weight; it had anchored her down to her left, and the rest of her body flung out awkwardly to keep her balance. Man, I wish I had recorded it because explaining how these people looked doesn't do it justice. Many people had the same sort of tipsy gait. Some even commented that I tricked them, but most were good-natured about it. Many people fell to one knee but recovered. Another woman picked it up quickly one-handed and realized that she was in trouble. She used her second hand to help with the weight, but it was too late and she fell right on her face! This next guy wins the award for best performance by an applicant. Here he comes for the last box. He did grab it with both hands but then bolted into a minisprint right into the wall...*crash!* (guy into wall)...*bang!* (guy into ground)...*boom!* (box into ground). I am thankful no one got seriously injured. For me it was just another day at the office.

THE SUITCASE-TEST SCENARIO #2:

This test had one suitcase on the table with cutouts on the side designed for applicants to insert their hands. The goal was to feel an object on the inside and then tell me what it was without pulling the object out through the holes and seeing it. The instructional speech was very long for this relatively easy task, but like the other speech I had to say it verbatim. Eventually I memorized it, so I looked into the eyes of the prospective employees the whole time while reciting it. I felt robotic as this speech was so redundant. I did my best to change the inflection in my voice and succeeded. I'll never forget the looks I got: bulging eyes, fear, and uncertainty to stoic, serious, and concerned. I got a few nervous smiles as well. The objects varied but included a comb, brush, screwdriver, cell phone, and a pair of scissors with dull blades. Very few people failed; I'm not even sure what the test was for. I can't imagine a scenario in which you wouldn't look at items during a luggage check. Maybe it was to see if people could follow instructions. Many actually couldn't, but they were probably confused by my drawn-out speech, which is totally understandable. I instructed them repeatedly but in different ways to "leave the objects in the box" and "don't remove the items from the box." I also told them over and over again to not verbalize anything but instead write it down on the pad provided. Yet, many people did the wrong thing on both counts, which I thought was funny. A person pulls out the scissors and says, "Scissors?" It was a judgment call on my part because he or she would fail the test possibly because I was using silly dialogue from the speech. Certain failures gave me some insight regarding the problem, and I felt obligated to level the playing field. Some were afraid to ask questions, so they jumped right into the test and failed. I would talk to them and explain what I meant by the speech, and all was well after that. In the end, there were a legitimate few who couldn't identify an object without looking at it. They might have been great employees but had to be cut.

I had a temp working for me at peak times. She was understandably embarrassed to read the speech to the applicants. It was definitely a painful under-taking. She actually yelled at me when I reminded her to read it verbatim. I ended up moving her to a different task.

A few months later, Anthony—another temp from my company—joined me. We hit it off imme-diately and had lots of laughs for the rest of our time there. One time he administered the feeling test. Anthony was black, and the applicant was white. Anthony explained to me that the guy had an angry demeanor. If Anthony could have read his mind, he's pretty sure the guy would have said, "I don't want this n— in charge of my economic well-being." We laughed about it afterward. To lighten the mood, I started using the names of famous people when po-tential employees walked through the door. It was a good icebreaker as many people were tense. "Hello, I'm Bill Clinton" (or George Bush or Tom Cruise—all the way down the line). I also starting branch-ing out, saying, "Hello, I'm Jennifer" (or Catherine or Amber). Some people didn't flinch, while oth-ers laughed hysterically. But in making people feel more at ease, my overall goal was achieved. Once, I spontaneously named myself and then introduced Anthony as "Madookoo." We started cracking up, though the applicant certainly wouldn't get it. I have no idea where I got that name.

Side Note:

MORE MONEY? OK

As I stated before, the management personnel changed frequently. One new manager asked if I wanted a raise. I said, "Sure." Perhaps he could tell that I deserved one. (I guess he was a quick study.) When he asked me to name my amount, I told him, "One dollar extra per hour." He replied, "How about two?" I accepted, but was I then supposed to say, "No, three"? This whole situation was strange to me. It was even more unusual that he asked me to call my agency and tell them that a raise was in order. So I called with him present, and he got on the phone and verbally verified himself. This was great and comical at the same time. Did my agency verify his credentials, or was it just too complicated due to the constant changing of the guard? Did they think I called them and used a made-up name and voice just to get a raise? Maybe so, but I'll never know. The manager shipped off quickly like the rest of them did, but I so appreciated what he did for me. It wasn't just for the extra money but that he quickly recognized something special in me.

Side Note:

CHI-TOWN

Another rotating manager and I were walking briskly together amid some chaos. When I asked him where he was from and he told me Chicago, I quoted one of my favorite TV series: "I first arrived in Chicago on the trail of my father's killers—" But he became agitated and said, "I cannot deal with this conversation right now." Maybe it was a bad joke, but I didn't even get a chance to explain. He moved on soon afterward to another city anyway, so no harm was done. Nevertheless, his reaction was golden.

Side Note:

LA-LA LAND

One of the rotating crews was LA based. It was an odd mix of employees. Some were extras in movies or performed various other jobs behind the scenes. Others had more significant roles, such as producing or writing. Since I was busy at work, I didn't get much time to ask as many questions as I would've liked. It was an exciting time nonetheless as Hollywood was in town.

November 15–17, 2002

Many of us temps worked for a major nature television station and magazine for three days. While visiting Boston, the company was having one of their periodic sales on all merchandise. Maps, atlases, and toy animals—among tons of other natural items—were on display. Our main duty was at the checkout counters, but we also did sales and customer service. I was put in charge of all the temps, and we had a lot of fun there. We were fascinated by the many different and unique products, which ranged from large globes to world atlases and magazines to travel gear and gadgets. I also enjoyed talking with customers and fellow employees about how our world is so thought provoking and diverse. Perusing the books and assorted earth-related items was an experience I'll always remember. We were given store credit at the end of the assignment, and several items were free! It was an unusual but very generous gesture on the part of the company. To this day I still support them.

December 8–19, 2002; September 16, 2003; December 5, 2003; January 2, 2004; January 26, 2004; February 17–20, 2004; March 8, 2004

I 've worked for an information-technology company seven times over the span of about a year and a quarter in Boston. Each time it was to either move around office furniture or set up chairs and tables for meetings. They had a huge storage room in the basement of the building; it looked like furniture was just tossed in there along with odds and ends. It was dungeon-like with its large, heavy door and musty smell. Plus, it wasn't well lit. When I finished a moving project upstairs, I had to rearrange the dungeon. Each time I worked for this company, I would have a crack at it, but only with a limited amount of time. I had a master plan and started organizing it from scratch, beginning at the back of the room. When I would return to the job again, the room would inevitably be altered. It was a challenge that I wanted to accomplish as my progress was apparent. I never did get around to it since I didn't get near enough time to do so. I was never sent back after the seventh time due to the timing of my other jobs. I hope it's better organized today as I laid the groundwork for it. One day was particularly brutal. I had to move some ridiculously heavy furniture with no equipment except for a dolly. Needless to say, I was soaking wet. When I finished, I asked my contact what she wanted me to do next. With my face dripping wet, I joked that moving everything was "no sweat" and that the water on my face was from the sink. She bought it, but then I told her that I was kidding. "You bet your life it's sweat!" I said.

December 27, 2002

My company consolidated two of our field-office locations. One of my managers asked if I could help him transport furniture for the day. Since the smaller items were already gone, it was just the big pieces that needed to be moved. It was very strange to work diligently with one of my bosses observing. He was pretty high ranking but still knew of me. My reputation had preceded me, which is the reason I was chosen. It was almost surreal as I grabbed furniture as I usually would, but in the presence of management. It was almost as if I was in the spotlight. That's how I saw it anyway. I made quick work of the pieces, and off we were to the other office to deliver. I got a surprise when we arrived. A very nice woman named Janice happened to work at that branch now. She used to work in the Boston office and had sent me on many of my adventures. We had a nice rapport going until she departed for this branch, which was closer to her home. We embraced and talked about some good memories. Another temp was working with her in the office. Janice introduced me to her as the "best temp in Massachusetts" to which the temp replied, "What about me?" Janice massaged her ego with comforting words.

Minibar Mishap minus a Drink

February 4–6, 2003

Several temps worked this three-day job. We unboxed brand-new state-of-the-art minibars for a company that specializes in automatic systems for these bars in an exclusive East Boston hotel. After that we transported them to individual rooms and then installed them. Well, wouldn't you know it? A percentage of the minibars were made improperly at the factory. The doors had been put on backward, which was a big issue because of the angle limitations of the cubbyhole that it fit into. No one noticed for the majority of the project since the first wave of units was fine; moreover, our job was to install it, not to take note of such things. As a result, we had to uninstall certain units and pack them up for alterations. We joked around about the fact that the minibars were empty upon arrival and that the doors just happened to be backward—just a little suspicious.

Temporary Marathon

June 20–July 18, 2003; September 11–12, 2003; September 23–November 9, 2003; November 24– December 2, 2003; April 16–May 4, 2004; June 21– November 30, 2004; January 2, 2005–January 11, 2008

This was by far the longest of any of my temp assignments. It was seven stints in all with the last and longest visit being almost exactly three years, with about nine months tagged on for the other combined stints. I bounced around several locations, but I worked at a college for the majority of the time. The company I worked for is an outsourcing specialist serving the business needs of a variety of companies and fields. These needs include records and imaging services, print services, mail services, and legal solutions. Some of their own employees were floaters, but on occasion the company would hire temps. I'll recount some of the memorable stories during my time at these locations.

COUNTERFEITING 101:
It never ceases to amaze me the number of times I go to a new assignment and earn instant personal trust. Sometimes it's detrimental to me. Not long after I

met the staff at one copy-center location, for example, an employee entrusted me with the techniques he was perfecting to counterfeit cash. He would use these high-powered color copiers and scanners, intended for company use only, for his own get-rich-quick scheme. Not only were the machines great, but an environment like that usually guarantees an assortment of the very best paper. He showed me some samples of his best work right when the boss was just about to enter the room. *Fantastic*, I thought. Being a temp often puts me in these awkward situations. I'm loyal to my company but have to at least appear to be loyal to the client. Since you're wearing two pairs of shoes, each step you take is magnified. I always try to stay clear of our clients' politics or people's personal issues. It's often impossible since you're expected to be a part of their team. Anyway, I eventually let him know in a nice way that I couldn't be involved with any felonious acts. He understood and with a parting comment explained that he was excited about a new type of bond paper the company had just started using; it was perfect for his "side work." I have to admit that the look and feel of the bills that he created were pretty darn good. He eventually got a job as a copy-machine serviceperson for a major company. Are you surprised?

COKE—AND NOT COCA-COLA, EITHER:

An employee shocked me while he was driving us from one job location to another in the company van.

He showed me the plastic bags of cocaine that he'd prepared and was ready to distribute. I didn't want to alarm him, so I acted nonchalant. If we had been pulled over for any reason, we would have been jailbirds. I'm glad he trusted me, but I was angry that he had put me at risk. We exchanged some small talk until we arrived at the location. Quarterly, we rented out some space in the college to Massachusetts state troopers for their meetings. Unbeknown to him, the troopers happened to be there that day. When I mentioned this to him, he said that although he didn't know they were there, he could smell them while he was preparing the cocaine bags in the bathroom stall. I wonder what would have happened if one of the troopers had accidentally walked into the stall.

I REALLY DIDN'T WANT TO HEAR THIS:

I did work for quite some time with a particular permanent employee, so I guess he felt comfortable confiding in me. We weren't even on the subject when he told me that he desperately wanted to have sex with his twelve-year-old stepdaughter. I suddenly felt like a priest hearing a confession. His manner and his low voice indicated that he felt guilty, not to mention the look in his eyes that said he knew it was wrong. I think he needed to get it off his shoulders and share it with somebody before he exploded or imploded— I'm not sure which. I thought it might do him, or the girl, good to vent a little. He elaborated somewhat, saying she's so beautiful with a great body. He even masturbated many times per day thinking about her. He'd had a tough life until recently, when he became a born-again Christian and then married into the lifestyle. I think this made him feel especially guilty about the whole thing. He mentioned, and I believed him, that he would definitely never act out on his feelings. He had a young baby with his wife and was busy with church activities. He was a great guy, and I'm honored to have known and worked with him during that time. I'm glad he confided in me and our conversation went well and in the right direction for him. I wonder if another person would have ratted him out, or worse.

THE SOUND OF MUSIC:

I was working with an employee who was blasting his music in our work area, when in walks a professor. What made it worse for me was the fact that the employee walked away, leaving me to take the blame. Not only was the music loud, but it was also vulgar. It was reggae, so most of it I couldn't understand. But the part of the song that was crystal clear was when they mentioned the female genitalia, over and over again. Of course the professor who walked in was female, so it complied with Murphy's Law. I turned the music off right away but in doing so looked like the guilty party. She didn't say anything about the music. There's no way she didn't hear it. When the employee came back, I told him what happened, and he just laughed it off. Another professional day at the office.

NINE LIVES, JUST BARELY:

An employee brought in a kitten one day and then sort of neglected it since he got busy. The kitten found its way up to a tall table and then jumped off. It was limping badly afterward. The employee took it away, but I hope he took better care of it after that. *Meow.*

ME AND JULIO DOWN BY THE SCHOOLYARD:

Strike one:

As I've mentioned before, employees often don't appreciate or want temps around, which was the case at this location. On my first day, I arrived early as usual. An employee told me that I could surf the web until management provided instructions for the day's work. That's what I did. Suddenly Julio, the assistant manager, pulled me around by my shoulder and demanded to know who I was. The other employee didn't say a word. Was Julio not expecting me, as he was the assistant manager? I told him who I was, and he said I couldn't use the computer again for any reason.

During one of my projects, I happened to be working behind a huge beam structure. Julio peeked around the beam at me and snarled, "What are you hiding?" I looked at him briefly and then kept working.

I would often accompany an employee to the neighboring buildings for deliveries. One early morning, he said he had only one small delivery and that I could wait on the bench in the yard and take a break to enjoy the weather for a few minutes until he came back. About a minute had passed as I waited, when Julio came strolling by. "What are you doing here?" he asked. As I explained, he seemed visibly upset and muttered something under his breath. That wasn't the end of it, though. A while later when I got back to the office, the manager summoned me for a private meeting. Julio actually complained to him, so I had to tell the whole story all over again. I was told to always go with the employees, even if they had nothing for me to do. This frustrated me as I always give the maximum effort for each job. Yet, I looked foolish and lazy for the wrong reason. Was I supposed to defy the employee and say, "No, darn it. I'm going with you anyway"? Politics! Well, three strikes and Julio's out. A few years later, I learned that a competitor bought out the company, which probably meant all of the employees were out and new ones were brought in with the new company. I don't wish anyone ill will, but I just smiled thinking about Julio's almost ten-year comfort zone coming to a crashing halt. Is he now somewhere where he has jerks treating him badly, just as he treated me? I guess I'll never know.

LIGHTS OUT:

A storage facility housed some of the college's items. There was a bathroom in the facility that had a light with a timer on it. One of the guys told me that once, when he was going number two, the lights went out. The distance to the light switch was far, and you had to practically crawl around a corner and fumble your way to the light, as it was pitch black. What do you do? Do you pull your pants up without wiping yet, or chance falling or someone coming in while your pants are down? Ah, life's difficult decisions.

IT'S ONLY FIVE DOLLARS:

I lent an employee five dollars, and he said he'd cover it when he could. I told him it didn't really matter, and he could take his time, as it was only five dollars. Every now and again the subject came up, and he always told me that he absolutely had to pay me as it was the bushido way. If not, he explained, he would have to kill himself. He was dead serious, too. What if my temp assignment had ended abruptly? He probably wouldn't have seen me again to pay me back. Would he have really done it? And with a sword to the midsection? I wondered. He did finally pay me, so I trust all is well.

MUSIC TO MY EARS:

One college I worked at specialized in music. I've worked at many colleges in different capacities, but this was, by far, the most exciting and energetic group of students I'd ever seen. Electricity was in the air as I meandered my way through the halls. Each room radiated thrills yet focus. It was great to witness; every few steps I took brought new, refreshing sounds from the instruments played by these talented students. Even the vocals coming from some of the rooms were phenomenal. The word "passion" doesn't do the school justice. The engaging conversations and willingness to share music samples spilled out into the hallways as well. I'm not sure if there is any school in the world like it. Rock on.

NOW TELL ME YOUR TRUE FEELINGS:

Some of the managers rotated between locations on an as-needed basis. One manager was particularly nice, respectful, and soft spoken. Every summer there were special programs at a different college campus that would partner with our college. We would deliver items such as college signs, posters, and the like as well as printed materials and other classroom necessities. On one such trip, I was accompanied by this quiet manager. As we drove the van along, he suddenly went berserk, ranting about all the things he hated about his job and the school in general. It was so loud that I had to cover my ears as he hollered with his eyes bulging like a madman. We are both white, so I guess he felt comfortable shouting racial obscenities, especially about the president of our college who was Indian. I said very little, as I felt stuck in the middle. I guess the open road allows many freedoms.

MISTAKEN IDENTITY:

We had a delivery at one location. I happened to be standing with the manager and the assistant manager, both of whom were Hispanic. The delivery guy walked right up to me for the signature. The manager commented afterward that the delivery guy automatically thought I was in charge since I was white. I know both of the managers were hurt by this, which is why I always strive to be the best example in race relations that I can possibly be.

THE SWORD IS MIGHTIER THAN THE PEN:

One of the branch managers was frustrated often by this one college employee. She was definitely annoying, so I empathized with him. One time, she called in a request. After he hung up with her, he just whipped his pen across the room and shouted obscenities. I calmed him down as we discussed what happened, and all ended well.

WIPEOUT:

One branch had its main door adjacent to the building's receiving area. I helped one of the employees pick up some mail at the post office while using the company van. As we pulled up to our building, the driver let me off near the entrance. I shut the door to the van, and all of a sudden the world looked like it was spinning. I slipped and fell on the ice, and since the driveway was slanted downward I began to slide under the van's tires. The more I tried to pull my legs out from underneath the tires, the more I slid under them. Luckily, the driver noticed that I had disappeared, so he had waited to step off the brake. I was holding a small bucket of mail with under my left arm, so when I fell on my left side the mail went flying in the air, too. There were some onlookers, so I imagine it looked pretty funny. I slightly injured my arm, with minor abrasions and pain. This was on a Tuesday, and we'd had some weekend storms that were never cleared away the day before, so I was angry. There was no salt or sand or any shoveling done at all. The injury could have been a lot worse. Since it was the receiving area of the building, you'd think it would be a safety concern. You could see and hear the trucks skidding and struggling up the incline and into the building. The snow, but mostly the ice, was about five inches thick and rock solid due to the property owner's negligence. It did turn cold on Monday, which solidified the snow, making it much more difficult for them to manage. I was sent to the hospital and told to take a few days off to rest my arm. I came back for only a day, and the area manager called and said my assignment was ending that day since business was slowing down. So after about four and a half years of many locations and adventures, it all came down to this? I'm pretty certain he didn't want any part of the responsibility of my injury, which was very minor. I respected him, so I didn't ask if our parting of ways had anything to do with the fall just a few days earlier. I was more than ready for the next adventure.

Life Is Full of Fun and Games

September 20-21, 2003

A few of us temps worked for an amusement rental company for an evening in Boston. A private party rented out several rooms in an exclusive Boston hotel for a game night. The games ranged from pool and darts to old, arcade-style video games; we had to unload these games and tables from a huge truck and then return several hours later in the wee hours of the morning to load them back in. Of course, once the hard work is done from setting up the games, naturally you want to test them out. Unfortunately, there was no time, and it probably would have been frowned upon anyway. The truck was on a really busy and tight street corner; we'd had some close calls with traffic while trying to haul down the big arcade video games. It was fun to see all the choices that they had. When we returned to load up everything, the party was just about over. They'd hired a gorgeous professional pool player to instruct or just play with the partygoers. She told me that she was still on the clock and wanted to know if I wanted to give it a whirl. I was most definitely game. We talked while having some fun shooting the ball around. We didn't play a real game, but it was great just the same. Alas, life can be fun.

Beat, Beating, and Beet Red

September 23, 2003

I worked for one hellish day at a department store in Boston. This department store, which is now gone, had me working with some of their files. More specifically, they had an office area where employees dropped off huge file boxes full to the brim with various files. My task was to bring all of them, about one hundred, to the roof. Each one was very heavy and bulky and difficult to get my arms around. I had to go up two flights of stairs and onto the roof and into a shed. That's right—shed. Whoever heard of a shed on a roof of a tall downtown building? Not me. It was brutal; I could bring up only one box at a time. Each step was a struggle, much less stepping over the stoop on the roof and all the way across to the shed. Not only that but I had to stack them pretty high in order to maximize the small amount of space. After the first trip, I knew it would take a superhuman effort to do the whole job alone. I kept on going and going, focusing 100 percent. I remember taking a water break and my heart beating like it never had before. There happened to be a mirror in the room. When I saw my face I was astonished. Man, was it ever beet red! I finished after some hours and though tired was satisfied at my epic performance. I just smiled when I thought about being told I was sent here to file papers. A few years later, I ran into a fellow temp whom I sometimes work with. He told me that he did the same job, but there were far fewer boxes and two temps. They lifted the boxes together and carefully walked up the stairs so as not to strain themselves. I'm happy for them.

Christmas Joy with a Little Sorrow Thrown in the Snowy Mix

Unknown Dates and December 4–31, 2003; December 1–31, 2004

I've worked many Christmas seasons for the United States Postal Service. It was usually for the whole month of December but sometimes more if needed. As previously mentioned, often is the case where temps aren't welcomed by a company's permanent employees. This was especially true at the post office. Temps are often seen as pillagers of employees' overtime as well as outsiders who just don't fit in. Also, many unions resent our inhabiting their workplaces. We often get dirty looks, comments under the breath, and even threats of physical violence. It was also commonplace to be sworn at in the most creative ways. (Geez, Louise. We're just trying to help and were sent in by your management anyway.) I worked at several locations, mostly in a large warehouse in an industrial area of South Boston. It was rented by the post office as needed. A yearly group of around one hundred temps covered the various shifts. We all worked pretty well together in a nice, open area, so if you didn't care for someone, you could just move on. We dealt specifically with the sorting of packages and boxes, with no letters whatsoever. Unfortunately, in such an open area, people usually stuck with their own skin color. There was racial tension that should have been addressed by management. I'm white, and I remember walking to an all-black sorting area to leave some packages that belonged there. I have no idea why, but I was being shouted at and called "boy." I had done nothing wrong, and even if I did, that was very harsh. I was reminded of slave stories from books or movies when the word "boy" was used to address blacks. Here we are in the twenty-first century, and it's the opposite? It was an unsettling situation. I just walked away; in that environment, it was an unspoken act of treachery to have reported such a thing. Our location was a long mile from the train station, so shuttle buses were provided by the post office. One day, I was the very first to arrive. As I waited for the bus, people started showing up in droves. The bus came, and as I was about to embark, I was pushed aside by a steady stream of black passengers that were very boisterous. The bus was then full to capacity, leaving me to walk. Now I might be late, and we were in the middle of a snowstorm. To make matters worse, the winds were whipping from the water. I made it on time but was soaked and frozen. I got some looks and a little laughter, too. I was understandably upset but didn't show it. These sad, negative race relations didn't change me. I know that there are only pockets of such nonsense and that such behaviors don't represent the feelings of the majority. Yet another time, I worked with one other white guy who was bad-mouthing blacks, using the *n*-word. Every time that we would work together in private, he would say the same sort of things, so I did my best to avoid him.

Side Note:

FACING MECCA:

Several large signs were posted, detailing the cities and zip codes in order for us to properly sort pack-ages. The packages were placed on different carts and then pushed to their respective areas. The signs hung about eight feet off the ground. So here we had twenty to twenty-five temps standing together with their re-spective packages in hand. Many had the classic deer-in-the-headlights look as they stared up at the sign, their eyes wide. It was a pretty daunting task in the beginning for most, as there were so many zip codes, which were eventually memorized. A few individuals just kept staring and staring, motionless. I wasn't sure if they were facing Mecca or frozen in a trance or what the deal was. I know some of them didn't read well, or were just plain lazy, but it was funny just the same.

January 20–22, 2004

I had a three-day job at a new medical-assisting train-ing facility in Chelsea where the finishing touches were still being done. I, alongside two other temps, unpacked and set up items for the institute, mostly geared toward medical-assisting students. The items ranged from medical equipment, such as stethoscopes, to mannequin models of humans complete with re-movable body parts. I recall holding and studying lifelike models of hearts, lungs, and—unfortunately— male and female genitalia. Most people don't get a good three-dimensional look at the inner and some-times outer parts of the human body. We also set up their phones, computers, and the like. Another inte-gral part to the institute's business was massage ther-apy. The three of us set up the very cumbersome and heavy massage tables just in time for our break—right on the tables. There were no students yet to give us a massage, but the tables themselves felt great on our lower lumbar after hours of physical labor. The tables also had a nice face hole for lying on your stomach.

One guy laid flat down on the table during his breaks, but when he got up it was slowly and deliberately. It was eerie but funny since he also had his arms folded over his chest like Dracula. It was an enjoyable three days as we revisited those tables often.

February 10–13, 2004; February 19, 2004

I worked alongside one other temp for this several-day job at a college in Charlestown. To this day, my coworker, Bob, is a close friend. This was a brand-new location for the western Massachusetts school, which branched out into the city of Boston. We helped un-box and set up many tables, chairs, and other college-room accessories. We built up tons of cardboard boxes as a result. Some of the giant ones needed to be folded so we could fit them onto a cart and bring them down to the recycle area. One time as I was folding a box down with my leg, I faked like I fell and slid down the box, and then I glanced up at Bob, who appeared shocked. He realized I was just joking once I smiled. In the recycle area was a huge cardboard-only Dumpster. Although it had the button to press to condense all the cardboard, it was still getting very full. We couldn't even fit anymore down the chute itself. There was a long metal rod supplied to us to jam the cardboard down even further. As I was jamming some down one time, I pulled the rod back and right through the wall!

I ended up having a conversation with the guy on the other side of the wall through the small peephole. As evidenced by the number of marks on the wall, it was always hit and at almost the same angle for who knows how long. Unfortunately, it happened to give in during my brief time there. Plexiglas was covering some other parts of the wall from previous mishaps. At any rate, we noticed a small Buddha statue on the lip of the chute. We commented on it, and it was still there a day or two later when we revisited the area. While putting some more cardboard down the chute, I spontaneously grabbed the statue and threw him down there, too! Bob paused and looked at me and said, "You killed Buddha!" We had a good laugh about this time and again as we'd mention it several times the next day or so that we were there. I didn't mean to offend anyone, especially Buddhists as it was just a spur of the moment comedic act.

April 3–4, 2004

One other temp had started before me on this two-day job. We worked at a Boston exposition center that housed a several-days-long food-and-beverage convention. Our booth represented a company that sold home carbonation systems along with concentrated, flavored syrups. As it turns out, there are many flavors to make your own soda at home, including the diet variety. I was thrown into the busy mix trying to hawk a product that I thought tasted gross and thus didn't believe in. I tried many varieties, but it left a terrible aftertaste. I am a real soda lover, like a lot of the population, so I couldn't be swayed by this cheap knockoff. There were some people who tested the product and seemed to like it. I wasn't sure if they weren't used to regular soda, or they were just being polite. Most moved on. The three permanent employees of course loved the product, or at least loved to have a steady job. The other temp was a nice lady, but I have no idea what she really thought of the product. They were all enthusiastic about the whole process, which they would demonstrate time and again. Fill the bottle with water, add the CO_2 fizz, and then pick a flavor. Repeat for the next passerby. They must have been on commission, given their enthusiasm as they approached people. It was so ridiculously over the top. I was waiting for them to break into song and dance. It was only cheap, crappy soda they were selling after all. The summit came for me as we participated in a little powwow designed to raise our spirits even higher. It ended with our putting our hands together and saying, "One…two…three…[insert company name]!" Boy was that painful.

May 5–June 16, 2004

worked at a government agency in Boston through another company for a little over a month, which is pretty unusual as it's mostly the company itself that will contact my agency directly. But it is a government agency, which is probably the reason for this rare course. The agency had lawyers who needed their closed case files organized, boxed up, and properly labeled so they could be shipped off to a remote location for safeguarding. The funny thing is, I'd heard about this huge project months in advance of me actually showing up on day one. There were never any specifics from my agency—just that there's a major undertaking coming up. Looking back on it, I wonder if it was hush-hush since it was government related. They were private legal files, it's true, but not nuclear secrets or anything. I think. Anyway, I could be totally wrong. Maybe the company simply didn't know enough about the forthcoming job itself or the dates. Fifty temps were to staff this six-month project.

I showed up and there was only one other temp who'd lasted for a few hours before getting nixed. Otherwise, it was only me. So I was going to do the work of fifty temps, and in only one month? I found out the allotted time soon after. That's exactly what happened, though. I'm just not sure why. Was I so good on that first day that they realized I could do it all by myself, and in much less time? They parted ways with the other temp in mere hours—because of me? This couldn't be true, or could it? I know I'm hyperfocused and all business, but this is ridiculous. I guess I'll never know, but I'm very proud of the job I did for them, and I found out they were more than satisfied as well.

Side Note:

HEY, I'M ON TV!

They had a meeting room where I would take breaks and lunches. One time I rested my eyes for a few minutes. I heard some sort of strange noise like electronic feedback, so I opened my eyes. To my shock, there were a man and a woman looking at me through the TV in front of the room! Come to find out, there was a canceled meeting that they weren't aware of. As for their initial silence, they probably wondered why the heck there was a sleeping bum in nonprofessional attire sitting before them.

Side Note:

BROKEN PROMISES

A lawyer named Greg was my contact there and was impressed with the results of my hard work and diligence from day one. Toward the end of the project, he gave me his business card and let me know that if I ever needed a reference to be absolutely sure to contact him. Not long after, I actually did need a reference as sometimes, even with temp jobs, clients require résumés and references in their selection process. I called and e-mailed him more than once, and he never responded. Through a contact, I found out he was still there. I was disappointed because he was so enthusiastic when he handed me his card. I'm not sure if he never responded because I was only a temp or for some other reason, but life goes on.

Comical First Impression

January 17–June 27, 2008; November 18, 2008–
December 20, 2009

On my first day at a software company in Charlestown, the receptionist told me to have a seat in the waiting area until she could locate my contact. As I was waiting, I watched the employees coming in and out through the glass door. To my surprise, I saw my old friend and fellow temp Bob approaching the door. He looked shocked but excited to see me. As he came through the door, he said, "Tom, Tom [last name]," and then he said "Remember me? Bob [last name]," as he spelled out his last name. Of course I remembered him, and we embraced mightily. He then took me to my contact. As we walked by, I joked with the receptionist—who witnessed the interaction—that this was the first time we had ever met and, as I'd hoped, she laughed at my little joke. Bob worked with and for me many times over the years. It had been a few years or so since I had last seen him, though. Coincidentally, it was just across the street at another company where we last worked together.

Several temps were working here, but Bob was permanent (to my surprise) and dismay (sort of). We'd talked about the many benefits and freedoms of the temp world many times before. He had his own reasons to become permanent, so I wasn't judgmental. I half-jokingly told him that I would slit my wrists before ever becoming permanent again in this lifetime. It was great to rekindle a lost friendship and to renew camaraderie with him in the workplace.

Bob knew my work ethic well. When he brought me over to meet my contact, Rick, he gave me the most flattering, humbling, unbelievable introduction. I was completely floored. The words he strung together put me on the highest of pedestals. It was as if he'd planned and written the speech and then recited it. I guess my reputation preceded me, even if it was by mere seconds. Was I worthy? It's not possible to take the humble out of me. I only wish it had been recorded, so I could hold on to the most fantastic compliments I'd ever received. I never realized that I'd made an impression like that on anybody, much less Bob. He was the quiet type but observed a lot it seemed.

As the weeks and months passed, Rick realized that Bob was dead-on accurate with his kind words. Rick also complimented me on my work and pretty much demanded that I be hired permanently in our conversations to which I digressed from the point. He was impressed by the over-the-top initiative that I always demonstrated. There was another permanent employee there that joked around with people, claiming he was "half man, half amazing." I heard him say it too from time to time. Rick asked me if I'd heard of the guy's saying, to which I responded yes. He then said, "You're not half man, half amazing. You're all amazing!" It was yet another unbelievable compliment. What is going on here? It's almost as if my modesty was being purposely challenged. Of course it wasn't, but it was so odd to be lauded this often and in this way. The difference with this assignment, compared to the others, was the dozens of projects that I was able to simultaneously sink my teeth into. Management and other employees noticed, hence all the praise. Rick got a good job offer elsewhere. As usual, one has to weigh the good versus the bad. I knew he thought very highly of me, but I was very surprised and humbled yet again when he told me one of the main reasons that he didn't want to leave the job was because of me! Wow, was I flattered! He was the manager of the department after all. And here I was—just a temp. His openness to my endless energy, suggestions, and project creation/completion was just a part of our great work relationship that I will always cherish. He did take the new job and is thriving, as I knew he would. I missed him a lot when he left. The excitement between us was gone. His replacement was terrible and not worthy of mention. I decided to leave sooner rather than later.

Strangely enough, there was a wild animal problem in the small courtyard of the building that housed the company. It was an urban area and the only patch of land around for several blocks that had any grass, shrubbery, or trees on it. Still, many animals persisted and called it home. I saw raccoons, skunks, rats, mice, feral cats, groundhogs, possums, rabbits, and even two American woodcocks, sometimes referred to as timber doodles. I'd never even seen these shorebirds on the beach, which makes this animal circus that much more unusual. You had to be careful when you entered the courtyard. You never knew what wild creature you'd see or have to flee from, especially if you were like me and arrived early when it was still dark. One morning, as I walked up slowly toward the entrance, I saw a baby skunk foraging in the grass. There was plenty of room between us, so I made a whistling noise and shook my keys to let it know I was there and would be passing by. It didn't react, so I assumed it didn't care about me, only its breakfast. I was wrong. As I inched closer toward the door, it looked at me and then growled and charged! I was shocked. It hadn't even noticed my approach. *My security badge better open the damn door today*, was all I could think. It worked and all was well with the world again. Usually, skunks will retreat and try to escape before they raise their tails to unleash their toxic fumes. I guess the baby ones haven't learned enough from their parents and are fearless. If I had been sprayed, would I have been compensated for the day(s) of my tomato bath and defunking? I hope HR would have been generous. An exterminator did finally come and for the most part saved our lives and those of the animals, too. I am thankful he was an animal relocator; I couldn't bear (get it?) to see our furry friends harmed in any way. There is still an occasional rat or cat roaming about, but otherwise all is safe again for all species concerned.

Trash Pickup or Something Else?

July 23, 2008

My job at a recycling company lasted several weeks and required several temps. For me, it was one day as I was plugged into a slot for that allotted time. The city of Revere had implemented a new trash pickup program. The company supplied each resident with separate barrels for trash and recyclables. The program had been in place for some time, but there was one small (and ultimately huge) problem to overcome. It was the reason we temps were patrolling the streets of Revere and placing leaflets at each residence. The problem was that the customer service phone number for the program was incorrect in the original leaflets. The original leaflet phone number was actually that of a phone sex line! You talk about damage control. Unlike normal trash collecting, this new program offered tiered reimbursement for recycling and was somewhat complicated. Thus, many people had questions and calls were a plenty. I can only imagine people's reactions—all age groups, ethnicities, personalities, and religions—who called the infamous number. It was another fun day as a temp.

Six Cents, Sixth Sense

September 11, 2008

The circus was in town, so temps were installed in different positions and time slots in Boston. I was there for one day. I worked in a private kitchen that served the performers only. I did various duties for the day, including washing and clearing off tables and cash-register work. I was covering for another temp who was the regular for that position. We weren't sure at the time if she was going to come back due to personal issues, so they invested some time in training me. At the end of the day, the manager had me count the cash and balance the receipts for the register. He explained that they were always off a bit daily due to human error. After all of my tallying, we were short six cents. "See?" he said. "We're always off one way or another." I replied, "I let someone go who was a penny short, and there was a nickel that I found hidden under the pile of cash." He smiled and was seemingly dumbfounded that we were exactly even. It was a first in his several years there. As I left, I told him that I probably wouldn't be back because the regular temp would return. This seemed to sadden him as my accuracy and attention to detail appeared to have floored him. Maybe it was his sixth sense kicking in?

April 9, 2010

This Friday-evening party was held at an exclusive Boston hotel. One of the function rooms was rented by either the university itself or some student groups for their graduation party. I was with one other temp as we worked for a subcontractor that supplied a particular brand of booze with their well-branded displays. We unloaded four casket-looking containers off the dock, brought them to the room, and had to figure out how to assemble the displays with little instruction. We returned several hours later when the party was winding down to disassemble the displays and put them back inside the coffins. I waited around in the interim in an adjacent room and inadvertently played spoiler to a few couples who thought they were entering a private room. Hotel management gave us permission to go inside while the party continued, so we quickly took down the displays and navigated the caskets through the blaring music and dancers (some of whom were almost clipped). So we danced around ourselves as we twisted and turned our way around everyone. It was most certainly a comical scene, judging from the looks and smiles we got (tainted with a little alcohol, I'm sure).

Navigation in German?

December 4, 2010

This fun job occurred on a crisp, wintry Saturday. I arrived at a hotel in Boston a little early, as usual. I used the house phone to call my contact, and while I was talking to him, he walked right up to me with his cell phone while smiling, which startled me. The day had already started with a laugh even before I started working for him. The company needed to track cell-phone signals in certain areas with the latest technology, so I was the chauffeur for the day. The three employees included one guy from Orange County, California; the other two were from the company's German office.

Off we went with the rental caravan. The conversations behind me were in both English and German as they were fine-tuning their processes. We ended up having two routes, one short and one long. They'd been to Boston/Cambridge many times, so they knew the routes well—and also their other location in Seattle. It's a good thing I knew the city well; they were focused on their laptops and just assumed I knew the routes. I didn't have any preprinted directions or navigational devices, so I had to interrupt them to ask about possible turns or forks in the road. I memorized the routes after each of the two trips. What if I wasn't familiar with the city? Multiple interruptions, maybe anger? I wasn't asked before we left. Anyway, we did the short trip three times and the long one, which was several miles, about seven or eight times. It was both humorous and mind numbing to keep arriving over and over again at this stop light, that billboard, this left turn, and that restaurant.

There was some small talk and some jokes as well. But the funniest conversation had nothing to do with me. After several hours, the quieter of the two Germans who sat way in the backseat by himself had the following to say after some computer frustration: "I hate computers! I hate electronics! I hate technology! I hate *everything!*" Following the rant, his fellow German jokingly chimed in, "I hate my life!" I was cracking up inside, and the situation was made that much more hilarious with their German accent. After eight hours without stopping for a break, it was over. We said our good-byes and dashed to the restrooms. I never asked if we could stop or whether or not it would ruin their research. I'm sure it wouldn't have, though. They probably just wanted to get it done for the day. I then gorged myself at Wendy's, since I'd had nothing to eat all day.

Side Note:

WHY ME?

During my morning commute on the train, a guy came on and sat right next to me, even though there were plenty of seats available. It's the only time this has ever happened to me on the train. I then ate breakfast at McDonald's, and he came in, ordered, and sat right next to me. Since I was a guy I thought the situation was funny. I can understand how these types of actions can scare women. After I finished eating at Wendy's at the end of the day, I took the train home. Just after the train doors closed and we were about to be on our way, guess who shows up? You've got it—the same guy came right up to the window and peered in at me. Was he a moment too late in stalking me? It was probably just a coincidence, but this just added to an already-funny and interesting day in which, it appears, I escaped with my life.

October 27–November 1, 2011

This driving job was a several-days-long excursion in the Boston area working for a telecom company. It was also to track cell-phone signals in certain areas using the latest technologies. This time I drove around a quite interesting and comical Pakistani gentleman named Danish. He was an electrical engineer and telecom expert. His company was a contractor for a major telecom company, which was comparing/contrasting cell-phone service only (no Internet) for three large telecom companies. It was a crazy setup in the minivan, where he had to wing it based on the van's interior. He had five laptops, ten cell phones (two for each laptop), and six GPS devices, all of which either had Velcro, were taped, or were tied down to be able to easily access or at least monitor the equipment. They were on the backs of seats, on the seats themselves, or just plain dangling. I think he did a great job.

I first met him where he was staying at the hotel in Saugus. He initially didn't greet me in the lounge area. He told me later that he thought I was a cop.

It's always interesting to find out about a person's first impression of you. It turns out he lounged in the hotel for more than three days waiting for me. He was lackadaisical and just took it easy for several days. His company was responsible for getting a driver, and he didn't care how long they took, as he was getting paid anyway. Still, that's an awfully long time to get a driver. I wonder how his company handled it and why they took as long as they did.

Anyway, we were off on many different random routes. It differed from my previous driving job, which had only two. This situation was much better, as we were not allowed to do the same routes and thus always had new horizons and conversations. We captured a ton of data because of our various paths. Sometimes he would get frustrated from all of the bells and whistles from the devices. I remember him saying, among other things, "Five laptops—you need a robot." There were constant chimes, rings, and alerts that he would have to attend to. The high-pitched sounds themselves were annoying to me too, but I couldn't imagine having to respond to all of them simultaneously, as it was certainly overwhelming. There were inevitably one-way streets, especially in downtown Boston, so sometimes we weren't capturing any new information. He would prompt us and say, "Come on, let's get some data," meaning "Let's find some different pavement." I'm not sure why he had six GPS devices. We almost always had new data, and I guess there were supposed to be backups to the backup GPS devices to ensure this.

Our conversational exchanges were many. Some were cultural, since he was Pakistani, and we sort of inevitably talked about 9/11. He thought there was a 70 percent chance that the US government was behind it. There was no animosity between us as we discussed this and other touchy subjects. We each took turns talking in a calm, unhurried manner. We certainly had the time to elaborate on many subjects. He commented on how ridiculous terrorists and their destructive actions are.

Of course, being two guys cruising around, we couldn't help but notice women who were out and about. I sort of had to be reserved in order to not give my agency a bad name. He, on the other hand, shouted out to women quite frequently. On occasion, we'd spot Muslim women wearing burkas, and each time he would yell out to them, not so loudly, "Terrorist." He would do it loudly enough so they wouldn't hear; it was just a joke for my benefit. It was both hilarious and surprising to me the first time and the subsequent times that he did this. I guess he was comfortable with me, as we quickly became friends. He recognized that

I would enjoy this odd piece of comedy with a Muslim calling another Muslim a terrorist. What made it funnier for me was that our exchanges were through the rearview mirror. He sat perfectly positioned in the middle of the seats for the best access to all of the electronics. By doing so, he inadvertently showed pretty much just his face in the rearview mirror, with all of the many expressions that come with it. It was almost like Skype or something.

At the end of day one, he had to send a USB flash drive to his boss via FedEx. We arrived at a location about two hours before they closed. We sat there for the two hours while he downloaded everything. He knew the place was closing and out of frustration said, "I can't download the information faster, dammit." The last delivery driver of the day came and picked up, and then they closed. After a few minutes, he finally finished downloading. "Murphy's Law," he joked, as we previously had a conversation on another subject regarding the law that haunts us all. The next day we drove by a bar in South Boston called—you guessed it—Murphy's Law. We were able to find another FedEx location in the sticks, so we made the deadline.

During our first few days together, his office kept trying relentlessly to set up his next assignment in

Atlanta. But they were only setting it up a day or two in advance, when he had many more to go in Boston. After hanging up with them, he would say in frustration, "How could you book my Atlanta itinerary when I'm still here?" It was quite a comical scene, as this happened time and again.

In one of the suburbs, we ended up on the top of a very steep hill. As we quickly glided down, I joked that the brakes didn't work. He wasn't sure whether or not I was joking...for a few seconds at least. I smiled, and he knew all was well. Later on in the day, we were driving regular speed, and the next thing we knew, we went flying into the air like the Dukes of Hazzard. It was brief but fun. Some of the equipment dislodged, and of course he wasn't wearing a seat belt due to the job constraints. He ended up airborne for a quick moment, but otherwise he was OK. He was totally shocked and wondered what the hell happened. We pulled over so he could get the devices back in place. It turned out that we hit what is called a raised intersection. I never heard of such a thing, as it's usually called a speed bump. I noticed the sign, but I didn't realize what it was until it was too late. It was yet another memorable experience of this several-day job. He works in Boston sometimes, so I hope to see him again and renew our friendship.

Side Note:

DOUBLE IMPACT:

I happened to be on a longer-term temp job at the time of this assignment, so my agency sent three temps to cover for me while I was gone for those several days. It's pretty ironic, I would say—hiring temps to cover for a temp.

The Mad Scientist

November 16, 2011

This one-day job was also a driving job. Coincidentally, I met my contact at the same hotel in Boston as I had for a previous company on another cell-phonedata-gathering driving job. I didn't have a phone number for him, so I asked the front-desk staff to look up his room number or company name. Neither one could be found. Strange! I decided to wait until the given time, as I was early. I waited in an area near the front desk so as to be obvious to him that I was there for that reason. Several people walked by, including a homeless-looking guy. After a smoke, that same guy came back in and inquired with the front-desk staff, who pointed in my direction. Right off the bat, there was something interesting in that I had to work for someone whom I thought looked homeless.

As we walked toward the minivan, he dragged his feet in ancient-looking, disgusting shoes that were so worn out that they appeared and sounded like sandals as he scraped his feet lazily along. *This should be a fun day*, I thought. One of the first things he asked me was, "Did you bring a book?" I was thinking that wouldn't do a lot of good while I was driving. I found out later that there would be some downtime, as this cell-phone research was a little different from what I'd been used to. There would actually be long breaks, and we would be pulled over, so I could read while he was working. He needed a similar setup as my Pakistani friend of the previous chapter. As he was setting up shop in the rear seats with all of the equipment, he asked me strange question number two: "Do you have a knife?" Of course I knew he needed it for the setup, but I was thinking, *Yes, I have a Rambo buck knife in my side pocket. I'm one dangerous temp, so don't mess with me.*

This time around we ended up having only one route. The route was kind of long, which made it a little more interesting, even though I'd see the same landmarks time and again. We did finally get moving, and his face also ended up being smack dab in the middle of my rearview mirror. He had me laughing under my breath the whole day, even though we hardly talked throughout the day. He had the overhead light on right above his head. With has disheveled look; long, messy hair; and crazy facial expressions, all I could think of was a mad scientist with lightning bolts going off in the distance—especially since he was laughing and swearing loudly on an intermittent basis. I guess the job stress was getting to him!

February 6–7, 2012

This was a two-day job for me at a newspaper, although it was a little longer than that for others. The free newspaper is given out at train stations, among other places, in major cities all over the world. We weren't handing out newspapers, though, as that was left to the regular employees. Our whole job was to hand out palm-sized booklets at train stations for a department store's David Beckham body-wear campaign. Easy enough—or at least, I thought it was going to be.

Our contacts preferred if we said, "David Beckham," while handing them out to grab people's attention, but saying the department store's name was fine as an alternative. With the masses of people piling through so quickly, we sort of naturally ended up shouting, "David Beckham!" faster and faster and over each other as well. This inevitably led us to saying, "Dackam," "Davidham," or any combination thereof. It sounded ridiculous but pretty funny as well. There were times when you happened to be handing them out alone because of employees' breaks or just to cover another area of a given station. During those times, you would say, "David Beckham," nice and clearly, since there would be no one else to mess you up, even if swarms of people whizzed by.

Here is the kicker—or the kick in the groin, depending how you look at it. The twenty-four-page booklet had extremely provocative seminude photos of David Beckham! He was shirtless on the cover as well as on some inside pages, and he was shown in various lengths of underwear all way down to only very small briefs! He had a lot of tattoos as well for those interested. There were also a whole bunch of poses, so you could choose your favorite. These were obviously ads for men to see the various underwear and T-shirt products at the store, but come on—let's face it. These ads were for women to drool at. I doubt many women brought their men to the stores to help them shop for said items. But what do I know?

It was superpainful to hand them out to guys of any age. Some thought they were cologne samples, and others thought they were handouts for a local tattoo shop. But many men were very offended and confrontational with me and took it personally. I heard varied comments from "I'm not gay" to "I don't like men."

Several opened the pages while walking and abruptly did an about-face, even though there was a sea of people behind them. They didn't care and most certainly didn't want to be disrespected or embarrassed. I had to calm them down by telling them it was just my job and that I handed them out to men and women; it was just some underwear to buy—that was all. I had to apologize some of the time too—all of this while working at a breakneck speed. I consider myself lucky not to get punched in the nose or worse. I don't know if female employees had the same problem or not, as I only worked with one briefly at a station. I doubt it, though. A man questioning another man's sexuality is always a problem. I knew as soon as I flipped the pages first thing in the morning that this would probably happen. It was just more widespread than I thought it was going to be.

The women, on the other hand, just loved the booklet. I heard, "Oh, David Beckham!" and "He's *sooo* hot," as well as other similar comments. Several ladies wanted two or more copies. I guess it might be to give to other girlfriends, but maybe they just wanted a pinup guy for work and home. Who better than David Beckham? There was a tiny chance they wanted to give it to their man, though (for shopping of course). But all in all, I went from being outgoing and making sure every single person had a handout to being very reserved. You must understand that my life was on the line—one well-placed kick from a martial-arts expert, and who knows? OK, my mind probably wandered. But I was reserved just the same. There were many men who laughed too, I'll admit. I'm very thankful for this. Regarding the actual physical part of handing them out, let's just say I was rife with technique—from the quick shuffle to my left and right and the 360-degree-spin move to the will-you-marry-me knee bend. I tried to make it fun for the people and myself too. Smiles abounded, for the most part. I even saw a skateboarder heading in my direction, so I stuck out my arm to smoothly complete the transaction. In the end I really didn't get a chance to ask any of the other employees if they had similar experiences, as we were separated as it got slower, but I'm sure they must have. I happened to go New York City the following week and was hoping they would have the same hand-out just for an alternative perspective, but there wasn't anything going on regarding ol' Davy boy.

Side Note:

EVEN EXCHANGE

I often give money or time to charities of all sorts. While handing out my booklets, I noticed a Red Cross worker looking for people interested in giving donations. He saw that I was busy, which is probably why he didn't approach me; I decided to seek him out. I gave him a booklet just for fun. He had a great attitude and convinced me (which was easy) to donate. To this day I have a set amount charged to my credit card each month. Life is great.

Side Note:

SUSPICIOUS MOTIVES

Just as with some of my more recent assignments, I had other temps covering for me on my longer-term temp job while I worked on this two-day one. What made the situation even stranger, though, was the fact that I handed out the David Beckham booklet to one of my coworkers on the long-term job. He was permanent with the company and passed by me at one of the train stations, so of course I gave him a booklet. He grabbed it and shuffled along with a curious smile. I saw him later on that day back at the ranch, and he asked what in the world I was doing handing these things out very early in the morning at a random train station. I like to keep a low profile and never reveal my secret temp adventures, so I told him I was just having fun. It's true that I was having fun, but I doubt he or anyone else could have guessed what was really going on.

May 1, 2012

This was supposed to be a two-day job for Alan and me, but it turned out differently for us than expected. I showed up a little before the schedule start time of 8:00 a.m. The place was locked since I was early. The next thing I knew, a very petite young woman showed up and sneered at me while saying, "Are you one of the temps?" I smiled while confirming this, and she told me right away in a nasty, loud tone that I was supposed to be there at 9:30 a.m. and to disappear for an hour and a half until she was ready. I apologized while leaving, and then I triple-checked with my agency and confirmed it was supposed to be at 8:00 a.m. We're flexible as temps, and sometimes schedules get mixed up by one side or the other. Her attitude wasn't OK, though. We were off to a great start.

The company we worked for one of a large conglomerate's subsidiaries. It was in a Boston design center that housed many high-end furniture stores. I showed up again at 9:30 a.m. and met up with my fellow temp Alan. He told me he was scheduled for 9:30 a.m.—go figure. Upon arrival the woman, whose name was Lori, didn't introduce herself. She told us throw our jackets in this little hole-in-the-wall of a closet, and she'd be right with us. We waited one full hour. Alan sat down, but I wandered around the different ultraexpensive showrooms and was shocked to see the prices of the furniture—an end table for $6,000, a coffee table for $17,000, and so on. I saw a large desk and joked to myself that it was probably $100,000. I looked at the price tag—$92,000! During my hour of perusing the items, another employee shuffled me off the floor so as to not make a bad impression for the clients. I was dressed nicer than some of the clients that I saw. Some wore only jeans and sneakers. How did that employee know that I wasn't a client as well?

Lori finally had us get some dollies, and we headed toward the loading dock. There was one other temp from our agency named Ian who worked there on a regular basis. He didn't talk much, but when I asked him how often he worked there, he told me every Tuesday. I found out later that that wasn't the case, but he did work there often. We started offloading furniture from the company truck; all of the pieces were totally wrapped up safely with Styrofoam, tape, and cardboard. She told us to be very careful, as the pieces were worth thousands of dollars each. We unboxed and unwrapped most of the furniture on the dock to minimize the amount of packing material that the clients could potentially see in the store, as it was definitely an eyesore.

As I started using the razor blade very carefully, I was told to be more careful. I was thinking, *Be more careful than I'm already being?* It'd be impossible, since you need a minimum force to cut through something. Anyway, the truck driver was also a company employee. There was no dock plate so there was a gap between the loading dock and the truck. Thus bumps and bruises to the product were inevitable during unloading. This is because he pushed the skids quickly and roughly onto the dock itself. Was this being very careful? Lori was belittling Alan and me from the get-go. She respected or at least tolerated Ian, even though he did things in a half-assed manner and compromised the furniture. Alan and I worked much more conscientiously but were still belittled.

After a trip or two to the third floor on the freight elevator, the situation started really getting ridiculous. Lori stopped the two of us and scolded us right there on the spot. "Just listen to directions! Just listen to directions! We do this every day, and you do not!" For some reason she really emphasized the *T* in "not," and her eyes bulged with this crazy look in them. She spoke in such a demeaning way, as if we were five-year-olds. Alan started to ask her what we did wrong. I interrupted him purposely and asked if he could help me with a particular piece of furniture. If I didn't do that, things were not going to go well, as she was just waiting for a standoff. We couldn't do anything right in her mind—even with me, as I demonstrated all of my years of experience and diligence on similar projects.

There were many different box shapes and depths. I used my hand to tear down the top of a particular box, since I didn't know how deep I could cut with the blade. She told me to use the blade as it was faster—as if I didn't know. If I used the blade in the first place, she probably would've yelled, "Don't cut the piece." I tried to say as little as possible, since it was a no-win situation.

Ian placed a desk on the wooden part of the dolly that was directly touching the desk, as opposed to the proper place onto the fabric. I pointed it out to her so the piece wouldn't be scratched, but she said it was fine. What if we had done it, though? Ian took another piece off the dolly, and I carefully guided the dolly with my foot as not to step on the piece. She said just step down on it. What if I had done that on my own? She would play mind games with dirty, demeaning looks here and there as well. We were cautious about opening of each and every box, since she was so very specific about listening to directions. We felt as if we were working in slow motion in a way, instead of regularly opening a box and moving on to the next one. She would just stare and glare at us. We asked if it was all right if we opened a given box, to which she always replied yes. This was the ultimate walking-on-eggshells situation.

There was a huge piece that we brought up. Alan and I decided on our own to work on it together, as Lori periodically worked in a different area from us and wasn't around. It was very obviously a two-man job to take the thick cardboard and so forth off the giant desk. The Incredible Hulk couldn't even do it alone. As we started in on it, she came back while sneering and very loudly said, "One person per box, it doesn't take two!" So we separated but eventually went back to the box, as it was necessary. I had to hold Alan back a few more times, as his temper was definitely flaring. I did it the same manner as before—by asking him for help with something. I'm sure she knew what I was doing, which is why things never escalated.

The summit of ridiculousness came when Alan and I placed a small end table in a designated spot. She noticed a giant crack in one of the legs. She gasped while shouting, "Do you guys just throw furniture around?" I was thinking, *Yes, usually for sport, but not today, though*. It was probably the driver who broke the piece with his rough ways, or else it was broken during the journey or even when it was originally loaded onto the truck. It most definitely was not us, though. There were also scratches and dents on other pieces of furniture that we discovered upon the removal of the protective materials, so obviously it wasn't us.

Afterward, we did some rearranging of furniture throughout the showroom floor. When we came to her to ask what she would like for us to do next, she turned her back abruptly on us and sweetly asked Ian if he would like some salmon, as there was a party downstairs. He practically blushed and said that he had to go. He was a temp just like the two of us—and even from the same agency. Were we not worthy of salmon? After only four hours, she told us that we were all set for the day and that she didn't need us for the next day. I saw her act so sweet to Ian and also to clients and coworkers. It was a Jekyll-and-Hyde situation, I guess, but I have no idea why. We did absolutely nothing wrong. I made a rare personal appearance at my agency after work to give them a summary of the day's activities, to warn them of any false liability claims, and to give any future temps that might go there a heads-up about the nonsense and mistreatment that would most likely come their way. I told my agency that I'd go back there to work if necessary—not only to avoid having another temp go through that experience but also to show my patience and perseverance in a tough situation. Not every client was nice by any stretch of the imagination, but this was by far the worst belittling I've ever faced on the job. Alan split so quickly afterward that I didn't get a chance to talk about things with him. I guess it's just as well, as he was in no mood to converse about such nonsense.

A Whole Lot of Holes and, Also Thrown in the Mix, a Bloody Shirt

May 3, 2012; October 25, 2012

This job started out bloody and ended up bloody—for me, at least. I purchased a brand-new high-end dress shirt that was—of course—white. I had just arrived at the location; while taking off my jacket, I accidentally sliced open my right thumb with the zipper. Blood splattered directly onto my right sleeve and also my midsection. Why couldn't I have worn black that day? Darn it!

I was in crisis mode when I cleaned up the midsection first, which went very well. At the time I didn't realize a bloodstain had the possibility of ever have being removed, especially on a white shirt. Since it was fresh, it came right off with water and a little scrubbing with a paper towel. Whew. There was just too much blood on my sleeve to remove. It was already beginning to settle in as a stain by the time I cleaned my midsection and got around to stopping the still-dripping wound. The best and probably only option was to roll up the sleeve, which I did. I was grateful that it was on the lower arm. Surprisingly, with all of the activity, I was able to avoid any further stains. What a great first impression that would have been. Hello, my name is Thomas, and I'd appreciate it if you would please disregard my little bloodbath.

While closing shop at the end of the day, I re-opened the wound while yanking extension cords up from being taped onto the floor. I shook my finger to get rid of the excess blood into a garbage barrel, which was thankfully lined with a bag. In doing so, I inadvertently got some blood on my left shoulder. The shirt's destiny was definitely not to remain white.

The life-science company I worked for basically connects vendors with the medical-research community in a trade-show format in Boston. I was with another temp named Michelle, and we met up with our two contacts, Alex and Kendra. They were both from Indiana, as the company was based in Fort Wayne. We helped out the vendors in many different ways, including carting their materials to and from the parking garage and sometimes even the street. Michelle helped out at the front of the room with registering and so forth. For me the bulk of the day consisted of punching holes into lunch tickets. Trade-show attendees received a lunch ticket upon entry. Each ticket had five circles on the face that vendors could initialize. The goal for the company was for each attendee to visit at least five different vendors. Attendees were supposed to have all five circles initialized before bringing their tickets to me. The big, exciting finale was me punching a hole with a hole punch in the ticket for the lunch workers to then serve up the free lunch. The hole was to signify that you had just been served lunch and could not come in line again—unless, of course, you restarted the process from the beginning and got a new ticket.

As always when there's a free lunch, there were vultures lurking. There were tons of food, so I was pretty liberal and hole-punched just about everyone's ticket—even though many had no initials on them whatsoever, much less the five required. I saw many people come through the line time and again and gobble down their food, only to return. Some of them looked and were probably homeless and just plain hungry. There was no way I was going to send them away and look at myself in the mirror at the end of the day. Alex came by every now and again to enforce the law. She sent many people away, explaining that they needed to visit vendors first.

Many people asked if the five circles meant five free lunches. It appeared as if not many people read the information sheet that they were handed along with the ticket upon entry. It clearly states the facts. I had fun with it, though. My responses ranged a lot. I sometimes said it was a trade secret, or I confirmed it was five free lunches but only if you could eat everything. Other times I hole-punched the card five times instead of just the required one; then I turned it over and said the holder could have ten free lunches, five from each side. I would punch holes in different spots on the ticket whenever there were two or more people that came together. They often asked why I punched opposite corners and so on. So I flipped the ticket over to its blank side and told them their interpretation of the placement of the hole was exactly what it meant. I got a lot of interesting and puzzling looks, but most event goers laughed and joked around just like I did. One vendor chose not to initialize circles but instead stamped a small tiger face. Every time I saw the tiger face, I would punch a hole directly in its nose. People loved that move. I made sure a good time was had by all in the food line on that day.

I showed up almost six months later for another round of fun. This time the two employees were Cecily and Meghan, and I was the only temp who showed up. It was the same routine as before, but when it came time to punch those holes, I was given a really tight space to stand squished next to a vendor. I told him that I was sorry to encroach upon his space. His name was Zack, and he was very happy that we were there providing the free lunches. When I asked, he told me that even though his company had very specific clientele, they were often too busy with work to come visit with him. Believe it or not, a free lunch was just the thing that flushed the people out from behind their working stations/cubicles. This included prospective customers as well. Free food was very often the only way to meet these new people. Even though doctors, scientists, and so forth were paid very well, they just needed an extra incentive.

The usual vagrants came through, and I let it slide. I tried to be a little stricter this time in fairness to the company. It backfired on me, though. I wasn't surprised, as I usually anticipate things from all my years of experience of reading different people and situations. I explained to countless people that we would like them to visit some vendors and get some boxes on their lunch tickets initialized *before* having lunch. In small letters on the bottom of the tickets, it said, "Visit suppliers of your choice, enjoy a free lunch, and get a free gift on your way out!" One guy asked angrily and specifically, "Where does it say that you have to visit the vendors before eating?" I just told him that I wasn't going to challenge him and to enjoy the lunch. Geez.

Many people said they already visited many vendors and were upset they had to go back just for a silly signature. I let them eat in peace. One woman walked right up to me and said, "I'm just here for the free lunch." Brutal honesty is beautiful, huh? I let that one slide too. There were so many foreigners who simply couldn't understand what I was trying to tell them. I explained things very clearly and carefully as well. I pretty much gave up most of the time, since it was obviously fruitless. When I said, "Initialize or signature," they sometimes grabbed a pen, signed the card themselves, and handed it to me, thinking they were doing the right thing. It was an eye roller, to be sure. How do these people get by in the upper echelon of society's great thinkers and problem solvers without the basic understanding of simple directions? I guess I'll never know.

Since Zack was right there, it was natural for people to turn right to him when I let them know that they needed at least one John Hancock. Then he'd sign the silly card, and they'd turn around and hand right to me. It was such a token. We had a lot of fun with it, though. He was more like a celebrity signing autographs for people than he was a vendor at a science fair. We would exchange views and laughs and talk about the many different and interesting ways the people approached me. The food was good, though, and well worth the comical shenanigans of the masses.

Cecily and Meghan had to catch a flight to the next city right away at the end of the day. They made this clear to me beforehand so I'd be prepared to rush. I had a cart down in the parking garage that I had used to drop off some materials for a vendor. I was hightailing it already to help the next vendor, with the cart in tow, and Meghan shouted, "Faster," which echoed down the corridors. For me to have gone faster than I was already going would have meant doing the one-hundred-meter Olympic sprint. The Olympics had just passed, so I wasn't about to do that; I just kept walking superfast so I'd be able to help out more vendors. A vendor parked in a garage across the street diagonally; I was worried about the repercussions, since it would take me significantly longer to accomplish this. I felt like I was walking in a speeded up film like Charlie Chaplin as I finagled my way with the cart through the busy street, spinning around and bouncing off the people, cars, and a few puppies to boot. I made it back, and Meghan took the cart from me and told me to get the hotel card and go fast (as if I'd been going slowly before). Before she could storm off in a huff, I said, "Hotel card?" I was thinking she meant her key card for the hotel room and wanted me to help her check out or something. Her face was emotionless; she was so stressed about the upcoming flight that she could barely speak and therefore practically mimed to me that she wanted the hotel *cart* that you put luggage on. I went for it and helped more people load up, and then the two ladies were on their way. I'm sure they made it to the airport with a little time to spare. Whew!

During the times I was using the cart, I had to press the handicapped button and wait several seconds before the door opened up so I might proceed to the elevator. There was a guy sitting right there at the doorway, staring at me. He seemed like he wanted a show, so each and every time I passed by with the cart and waited for the door to open, I simply improvised. I did some Chaplin-esque moves at times and danced creatively at other times. He did enjoy the show; he laughed each time, but he finally left, as did my practicing improv techniques.

Roll Out the (Multicolored) Carpet

May 11–12, 2012; October 29, 2012; October 31, 2012

I visited this job a total of three times in span of just over five months. A major department store had an annual Persian carpet event held outside of their store in a huge rented tent in Chestnut Hill. It lasted for a few weeks and used plenty of temps to cover the various shifts. I only worked a few shifts this time around. I helped with unloading and laying out of the carpets for display. During the actual event, the temps assisted in showing the carpets and rolling them up in order to bring them to the customers' vehicles. As we removed the inventory, there were only empty pallets left, which we would stack to a height of about six feet. At that point, someone came along with a forklift to easily transport them to a different location.

Well, wouldn't you know it—one temp decided to go way above the agreed height and was throwing the pallets ever higher atop the pile. Why? I don't know. Maybe he thought larger piles of pallets made more sense. It was a dangerous situation at best. There was very little supervision, as with most jobs when there are a lot of temps. As the temp threw one pallet even higher, the inevitable happened—it came down crashing right on me! I was working on something else but was also keeping an eye on him for just this type of situation. The pallet bounced off my right side, hitting my hip and ribs. It hurt a lot but not enough to warrant a hospital visit or anything. Thankfully, the ground helped break its fall. The other temp blamed me for the mishap and said I should have gotten out of the way. Fingerpointing? Could this have been the first time in recorded history that finger-pointing has ever happened? Worse than the physical pain, I was pained by the fact that these ridiculous and risky things still go on in today's sophisticated society. It could have been a lot worse, to say the least.

I have worked for that company two more times since then, only in their regular store in the mall. On the first day, we were sent home after only a few hours because of Hurricane Sandy. We took the next day off and then came back for one full day, which happened to be Halloween. Edward, Sean, Leroy, and I met up with our contact, Thomas. There was basically a lot of fixture work that needed to be done. We moved plenty of racks, hangers, and displays of all sorts from different parts of the store and to their other location on the opposite end of the mall. It was interesting to see all of us parading around in our required black shirts and pants. It was especially funny when each of us had to cross the length of the mall one behind the other with our respective rolling racks. The train of rolling racks was just about to leave on the across-the-mall journey when I noticed a permanent employee right behind me. I asked her if she wanted to be the caboose, but she smiled and declined, saying that her work station was right here. As we departed, I turned to glance at her, and she had this longing look in her eyes for our impending journey.

As Thomas, our contact, led us on the way to one of our tasks, we happened to cross paths with a woman he clearly didn't like. Previously he was the nicest and most soft-spoken guy you could ever hope to meet. But suddenly he muttered curse words about her; then his voice increased in volume, and he said, "Where's the sledgehammer?" It was such an odd and briefly tense situation. Fearing the worst, Leroy quickly spoke to him in an effort to make Thomas calm down. It turned out that the two sets of comments made by Thomas were unrelated—thankfully. We needed a sledgehammer for a different reason altogether. The rest of the crew didn't say anything at all but obviously would have taken action if necessary. It did seem exactly like he meant to hurt her in those several seconds of harshly spoken words.

He also most definitely appeared to be a Jekyll-and-Hyde type. This whole situation lasted less than a minute but was very frightening to us. Even so, just as quickly as it ended, it started to become funny. After Thomas left for a few minutes, we just laughed and talked among ourselves about the incident. I guess the poor way he spoke of her was just office politics at work.

We needed the sledgehammer to smash down and break apart an old display fixture in the back room that was to be discarded. It was funny that the display fixture itself weighed a ton and could barely be budged by three large men, and yet it displayed only super lightweight women's hosiery. Go figure.

THE DARK-ABYSS SCENARIO #1:

We threw away the broken fixture pieces and other debris into the large trash compactor that was in the receiving area. We would walk up to the lip of the compactor and heave any trash we liked right down into the hole. The problem was that there was only one tiny lamp showing the way to the lip. We could barely see as we tiptoed to the edge, sometimes with very heavy items in tow. One false step and good night! But the good thing was that at least you couldn't be compacted until and unless someone pressed the button.

THE DARK-ABYSS SCENARIO #2:

There was an ancient-looking trailer that was attached to a loading dock to increase the amount of storage space in the building. For the most part, it stored bags of all shapes and sizes, both paper and plastic with their store's name and logo on them. Since Thomas had extra help in the form of us temps, he decided to at least attempt to reorganize the trailer. Once again it was just one tiny lamp that was being used to see all the way down the thirty-foot-plus trailer. It made especially hard to see in there, since there were different piles of bags jutting out at certain points. There were spider webs all over the place and it stunk of mildew as well. A lot of the bags were ruined because there were plenty of holes and cracks in the ceiling through which rain and snow had dripped. There were many trips in and out of the trailer for the various tasks that we had in there. Whenever we trekked out of the trailer, it seemed as though there was light at the end of the tunnel. But then we had to trudge right back in. Ultimately there was light at the end of the tunnel—but I would've ponied up the cash for better lighting in both cases.

The Never-Ending Lunch Break

June 28, 2012; November 9, 2012

I worked for this company twice in a period of just over four months and in two locations. About twenty of us temps were mobilized to work for a hospitality company. It was at a college's dorms in Cambridge. We had to replace the vast majority of their mattresses and box springs with brand-new ones. We also took away the old ones, a task we naturally did first. All of our teams worked in conjunction well with each other as we systematically went floor by floor and building by building for removal. We first laid them onto the sidewalk; soon after, the truck showed up, so we loaded them in, and off he went.

As you could imagine, some of the mattresses were beyond disgusting—complete with piss, blood, sweat, and other unmentionable fluid stains abound (some were still wet!). Most were just plain filthy, with dust mites, dirt, and hair, which I personally can't stand. I was glad when that part was over and we had moved on to the nice, new, clean mattresses and box springs. I couldn't wait to get started so that we could finish sooner and go home to shower those bodily fluids off us—not to mention the fact that it was very hot out, so we were soaked with sweat. But there was no way it could go quickly, as we had to wait a bit for the new stock to arrive. Our contact, Ralph, told us to just relax, hydrate, and take a half-hour lunch, during which time the truck would arrive. We wandered back from lunch and noticed there was still no truck. Boston is a very compact city with many one-way streets, and it can be very hard to navigate even for the residents. But if you're from out of state, which the truck driver was—well, good luck. Ralph was on the phone with him often, doing the best he could while using his smartphone to help the driver navigate. Didn't the driver have directions or at least a GPS? He must have, but I guess we'll never know for sure. We ended up taking a four-hour lunch! All the while, those bodily fluids from the mattresses had plenty of time to dry up on us—eww. At this point most of the crew was so tired from the morning's work and then the very long bake in the sun that they were just spent. But we had to push on with renewed energy, since we had many hours of heavy labor ahead. It was another day for the books indeed.

I worked for this company once again in Braintree at a hotel. Unlike the previous college dorm, this hotel was sort of unique in that it housed many long-term residents, most of whom were under government-housing umbrellas of some sort (such as section eight). We were very careful not to disturb residents, even though they had prior notice that we were coming. Many had small children. We did basically the same thing, except this time we were required to remove the bed skirts, put them back on the new mattresses, and put mattress covers on the new mattresses to block any bedbugs from a potential infestation. Before we worked that day, we were told by our contact to never utter the word "bedbug." If it came up, we had to just say, "BB," and he would know what we meant. He told us that his company could be open to complaints and lawsuits otherwise. I'd say it was another interesting day at the office.

Humpty Dumpty Sat on a... Chair, a Fruitful Conversation, and Other Various Stories

November 13, 2012; December 5, 2012; March 11, 2013; April 9, 2013; July 16, 2013; August 13, 2013; September 10, 2013; October 10, 2013; October 29, 2013; November 12, 2013; December 11, 2013; January 28, 2014; March 11, 2014; May 13, 2014; June 4, 2014; June 25, 2014; August 19, 2014; October 21, 2014; November 12, 2014

''ve worked nineteen times for this company in a span of almost exactly two years. It specializes in holding conferences for specific business subjects that improve the education for management employees in a multitude of industries. It's held at a Boston hotel. My contact, Jay, worked for my agency as a temp decades ago, which is where he got the idea of calling for temp help himself. The circle of life is interesting, just as the circle of temps is. I hesitate to write the first part of this chapter because it seems like I'm poking fun at someone. I don't judge people in any way at all. Sometimes we all make observations, comical or otherwise, or just find ourselves in unique, spontaneous situations that we react to accordingly.

On my third visit there, one of the conference attendees looked exactly like a real-life Humpty Dumpty, with suspenders on and all. I never saw anybody so perfectly rounded. Unfortunately, the chairs for the attendees had arms on them, which prevented the rotund gentleman from being able to fit in them. The only other type of chair the hotel had available was a very small armless chair that could only possibly hold one of his cheeks. He accepted it and was glad to finally be seated. It was about this time that my contact said, "There's a chair for him," while pointing around the corner. I took a look and saw a bench in the corner that could have seated three people. I had to laugh and shake my head. It was my gut response, and there was no harm done to the guy. It was a private joke between two guys and nothing else. I would never go out of my way and deliberately poke fun at anybody for any reason. I wanted to clarify that for anyone who may look negatively at my story. I feel like there is room in this world for spontaneous jokes as a stress breaker at times. But any brief private joke or comment I make or partake in would never to be brought up to an individual so that they may believe they're on the receiving end. Enough said. I'll just mention that when the lunch buffet began, the guy was first in line. No joke.

It was during my fourth visit there that I overheard something comical. I know hearsay doesn't hold up in court, but here are the details from the conversation that I heard. The speaker at this particular conference was English. During a break (during which he ate an English muffin, interestingly enough), an attendee came up to him with a comment. She was concerned not for herself but others. She mentioned that in America he might not want to use the word "fruity" but instead maybe "fruitful" so as not to offend the gay community or others concerned about their feelings. I couldn't quite hear the rest, since others were talking in the area, but it sounded as if he was going to oblige her wishes and was apologetic. All of this fruit talk made me decide to go enjoy some of the fresh fruits, fruit bars, and even fruity jelly (on an English muffin, of course) that was on display in the break area.

On my fifth trip, I was doing the usual laying out of name badges for the attendees. Upon arrival at the check in table, attendees would look in alphabetical order (first by company and then by last name) for their badge. The badges, which were perforated stickers, could simply be peeled off and stuck on their chests. As I tore off and separated them from the sheet, there was inevitably some paper left over from the sheet that adhered to the badges themselves. Most badges were square in shape, but many had odd pieces stuck on them, so the badges didn't look quite perfect when they were spread out—especially since they were white laid down on a black table covering. With around one hundred to lay out, I didn't have enough time to tear off every little piece or imperfection. Besides, once attendees peeled the back off and put the badge on, the imperfection was discarded along with the backing of the sticker.

Anyway, some shapes were sort of weird looking, but one took the cake—devil horns! When I laid out this badge, I knew I had to remove the horns, which were coincidentally very evenly placed above the badge. I tore them off as evenly as I could, since there were no scissors or anything. If not, I wonder what the attendee would have thought or even noticed. Would he have felt cursed? Most likely he would have just peeled the back off (with the horns intact) and discarded it without even noticing. These minor things just bring a smile to my face when I recall them fondly.

My eighth visit brought some interesting things to mention too. The event happened to be a women-only leadership conference. While my contact, Jay, and

I were chatting it up, I asked if there were any men-only conferences. He told me no, since the men were often the majority of people in the meetings anyway. This got us to joking about the potential of white-only conferences or Muslim-only and so forth. It was a funny break from the usual quiet voices that we used in such a professional environment.

The tenth visit brought us a briefly unhappy attendee. As soon as she picked up her badge, she angrily told me that she wanted a new one printed out. We didn't have the capability to do so right on the spot, as the badges were printed back at Jay's office. It turns out that Jay misspelled the woman's last name, which was Hughes; he forgot the second *h*. So this woman saw just her first name and "Huges." We gave her a blank badge to write the correct spelling on. She calmed down quickly and explained to me in a low voice that although she was average weight now, she was once very big. This led to her overreaction—as if we knew she used to be heavy and thus typed her name incorrectly on purpose or something. It's so crazy how all of the hundreds of name badges were perfectly typed and double-checked monthly, and the rare error just happened to be in this exact situation (Murphy's Law strikes again).

It was during my fourteenth trip that I almost witnessed total mayhem. Both Jay and I happened to eat our lunch with the speaker. Jay sometimes ate in the conference room with the speaker or attendees, but it was very rare for the speaker to actually join us outside of the room at our registration table. Anyway, after the speaker finished talking with us and eating, he decided to take a walk around the building, stretching his legs and talking on his cell phone. Well, the next thing we knew, many upset attendees approached Jay and me and told us the speaker still had his microphone on while saying derogatory things on his cell phone about the attendees themselves!

We were in damage control, to say the least. I thought I saw him walk downstairs, so I pursued him to let him know—when suddenly I bumped into two more frantic ladies who told me more of the same. I couldn't find him, so I rushed back upstairs and luckily found him before anyone else did. I whispered the emergency situation to him. He was pretty stone-faced, but you could tell by his eyes that he must have said something pretty bad. It wasn't our first thought, but while I was looking for the speaker himself, Jay realized that all he had to do was turn off the volume from inside the conference room's speakers. I informed Jay that I talked to the speaker, and the next thing I knew, lunch was over and the speaker was just beginning his afternoon presentation. Jay slipped in the room to see what might have been said, and there was no mention whatsoever of the whole dramatic situation! We were totally perplexed as to what he actually said on his phone. During the afternoon break, none of the attendees complained or said anything at all regarding his major flub. To this day, we are dying to know what he said; if it was so upsetting to so many, it's surprising that that was the end of it, just like that. This could have been a major disaster for not only the speaker's reputation but also—and more importantly—to Jay's company and all of its many dozens of fantastic speakers. I couldn't believe it, but during the next critical few weeks, there weren't any e-mails whatsoever on the subject at hand. We just wiped our brows and took a deep breath.

It was my fifteenth time there when I had a personal showdown—only I didn't realize it was a showdown until it was over. During a brief lull, I happened to look across the hallway into the entrance of a doorway that led to the kitchen. A leaf blew in right into the doorway. I thought, *That's weird since it isn't the fall or anything, and we are up on the second floor, anyway. Where did this leaf come from?* I stared at it for a minute or so and decided to get a closer look. As I approached, the leaf ran! I found out later out that there was a mouse problem in the hotel. I guess I lost the showdown at the mouse corral, as that little mouse outstared me until I couldn't take it anymore.

My sixteenth visit there brought yet another unexpected situation. It was another women-only conference. As I was signing the women in, a man walked up to the line! I recognized him from a previous regular mixed conference. We looked at each other a bit awkwardly, but I signed him in as well. The conference's name was such that it was obvious that it was intended for women only. There is no way that he came in by mistake. Nearing lunchtime, he let me know that he'd be back in about an hour. When I saw Jay next, I told him that the man would be back in an hour, but I joked it was because he was going to change into his skirt, get some makeup, and so forth.

Trip number seventeen had something worth mentioning too. Based on the look on her face, I guessed an attendee might have an issue. I asked if there was something wrong and if I could help her with something. Although she looked hesitant, she asked if I worked for the hotel. I told her that I worked for the education company. She then whispered to me that the bathrooms had run out of female supplies. I let her know that I would alert the hotel staff that minute. I did so, and a bit later she came out of the conference room. I said that she was all set now, as I knew that it would take no time at all to refill the dispenser. A minute later I happened to see the hotel employee whom I had notified about the situation. I casually double-checked with him about the restocking of the dispenser. He said that back in the day they refilled it but not anymore. I had jumped the gun and told the attendee something that was incorrect. Dang it.

I quickly went to the restroom area and waited a few minutes to apologize to her and then go to the drugstore for her, which was about a five-minute walk away—especially since she was limping pretty badly. It was too late. She had already went to the drugstore and come back soon after—in a great mood, understandably. I did apologize and thought she might be upset after the misinformation she received from me and the limping combined. Thankfully, I'll never understand the trouble that women experience on a monthly basis. Also, even with this embarrassing situation in mind, I'll still always go out of my way to try to help someone in need.

Visit number eighteen was sort of official. During a break, one of the attendees saw me standing at my post as usual. She asked, "Is this your official job?" I took that to mean standing there at attention and doing nothing else. I told her it was my unofficial official job. She laughed at my response. Of course she had no idea that I was a temp, so that made our little conversation that much more interesting.

November 30, 2012

We had an army of temps for one assignment on a Friday evening. We were working for an IT services company in a downtown-Boston brokerage-firm location. We waited patiently for the market to close at 4:00 p.m. and then allowed time for employees to vacate their cubicles and other working areas. It was time for them to get new computers, even though they already had what appeared to be new computers. Pretty soon we'll be going backward, I suppose. I'm guessing that the brand-new computer models will already be produced and ready to distribute before we set up our current "new" ones. How about we skip two or three models and just jump to the fourth one?

Anyway, our whole temp army was dispatched to do a military-style operation. We covered nearly every square inch of the many floors that needed removal of the computers, keyboards, monitors, and, of course, mice. There were so many worker bees that it was overkill, but that was the goal of our contact—to be done as quickly as possible. Come Monday morning at 9:30 a.m., there could be no room for error with all of the trading and so forth that had to be done. After this task was done, we had teams right behind us who were responsible for the installation of the new computers. All of the important IT work was to be done by the company later that night and over the weekend to meet the impending deadline. There were some employees still working in their cubicles here and there. We were instructed to just leave their computers alone and to get back to it at a later time, after the employee left. In one area there happened to be several women working together at their stations. They turned around at saw the huge group of us coming right at them. I'm sure they knew we were coming, but maybe they were surprised at the sheer number of us, as one of them said, "It's like an invasion." In their nice, quiet work atmosphere, I can definitely understand what she meant. They were good-spirited about it, though, and joked around a bit with us. There were most certainly some scary-looking guys in the bunch. I hope I wasn't one of them. It was Movember, which is moustache month, and a guy who was working with the women asked if that was the reason that I had a moustache. Before I could answer, one of the women said she knew that wasn't the case and that I had a veteran moustache. I'm glad she noticed.

January 16, 2013

This one-day job in Medford was supposed to have me assisting with some merchandising and display on the shelves of a supermarket. But it was a different story altogether. I met up with my contact, Waleska, and for some reason she wasn't happy to meet me. I extended my hand and introduced myself, with no reciprocation. She barely looked at me and said, "Did you ever do planograms before?" I barely understood her thick Spanish accent. I told her that I had limited experience and that I wasn't an expert or anything. She seemed miffed when she said, "You don't know how to do it, then?"

I said, "Just show me what you would like done, and I'll happily do it for you." She wanted to talk to my company's office, so I connected her to the woman who sent me there. Luckily, she was also a native Spanish speaker, and both parties were from Puerto Rico. I hoped this would help clarify our situation.

It didn't at all. Waleska seemed to be grumbling, and when she hung up the phone, she asked me the same question: "Did you ever do planograms before?"

I had no idea what was said on the phone, so I was a bit hesitant. I was walking on eggshells when I told her, "Sort of…" She got mad, raised her voice, and told me the lady on the phone told her that I had done it before. This was ridiculous from the beginning, to be sure. She then impatiently handed me the planogram, which was around twelve to fifteen pages long, and said, "OK, now do it." She stood there and watched me to see if I knew where to begin.

So there I was in a huge aisle with a planogram that was both text and box based. It included dozens upon dozens of shelving units, with some chicken scratch written here and there, as well as other random things being crossed out in it. I had the same question as when we started. "What would you like done?" I know she handed me the stupid sheets of paper for her own satisfaction. She probably just wanted to pat herself on the back since she was such an "expert" on the subject. She finally did show me what she wanted done—in such a token way, though, that it only took about twenty seconds. I read and understood quickly and was working on a shelf, but naturally I had questions. I wanted do the best job I could for her, but she wasn't allowing me to. She passed by my aisle soon afterward, so I grabbed her and asked a few questions. She gave me short answers, though. Not long after that, the store manager came by and asked the inevitable question: "Have you ever done this before?" I told him yes but not for years. He walked away, and a few minutes later, Waleska came to me and told me that she was sorry that she couldn't use me for the day.

What the heck? She sicced the manager on me? Was I on a hidden-camera show? It turned out that there were many other temps and locations that did the same project that week. Was each temp an expert in planograms? I think not. I was there for barely an hour. I could already understand what I was doing as I perused the booklet. I was just trying to fine-tune the process the best I could with hardly any help from her. I'm pretty sure I was the only one sent home from the project, as my contact had a negative attitude from the get-go. This was unusual in the temp world, as most contacts loved any and all help they could get. I'm very confident and have a ton of pride, and I was pretty outraged and offended as I left. However, I smiled, apologized to her, and told her that I wished I could have done a better job for her. I called my company's office to update them on the situation. I talked to the same lady, and she was equally upset; she decided to bring it to the next level and let her manager know. I never found out what happened. I'm sure nothing came of it, though, as it was probably an isolated incident, and as always the big picture is what is important.

Mirror, Mirror, on the Wall, Who's the Humblest of Them All?

February 1, 2013

Several of us temps were enlisted to work for a rug company at a department store's Persian rug sale event in Belmont. This was a different company and city that I worked at than in a previous chapter that I'd written. We did various setup tasks for a while. The next thing I knew, I was stopped abruptly by Jose while pushing a heavy pallet of rugs, which is never a safe thing to do. Our contact, Jose, and I were inside the back of a tractor-trailer at the time. He told me that he was very humbled that temps would come to work at a given assignment at the drop of a hat, even it if meant traveling far distances to unknown locations for very low pay. He told me that he valued his job and couldn't imagine what we temps went through on a daily basis. He looked like he was ready to cry; he had a pensive, faraway look. He went on to explain that he had had a drug and alcohol problem for more than twenty years. He was now clean and sober, and most importantly, he had found God. I was the one who was humbled by all that he confided in me in that chilly trailer on that day. Ultimately, he stopped me in my tracks literally and figuratively. That's the one and only time in my temp career that someone ever remotely offered kind words or acknowledgment of any sort regarding what temps routinely go through.

Gone in a Flash...

September 19, 2013

I worked for one day at a conference for civil engineers at hotel in Cambridge. It was actually for only a few hours in the morning. I had to set up shop, organize the handouts to the attendees, and so forth. My contact told me that I was free to go after the last attendee showed up and signed in. There were several different kinds of conferences going on that day, so of course there were different employees manning each of the doorways just like myself. My last attendee showed up and went into the room, so I packed up the few belongings of my contact as I was instructed to do and put them neatly under the table for him. I was just about to leave when the woman manning the door directly across from me rolled her eyes and said, "It's going to be a loooong day." At this time it was only 9:30 a.m.

She asked me when my day ended, and I said, "Right this second," as I turned and sprinted as fast as I could down the long hallway and around the corner, until she couldn't see me anymore. I have no idea what she thought, but I hope she enjoyed my little show. My guess is she thought I was kidding and that I'd be right back. I did it for fun, but also I had extra energy, as I was excited to get out of there much earlier than expected. That enabled me to secure the next job that was waiting for me, which started about an hour from then.

Survey Says: Don't Threaten Me

September 25–26, 2014

I worked for two days for a survey company at Boston's South Station bus terminal. My job was to hand out surveys with pencils to passengers who were waiting in line to board their respective buses. If they finished the survey before boarding, I'd collect it. If not, they could simply drop it into a mailbox. We just needed to collect data in order to improve bus service for the northeastern corridor. Passengers would ask me questions at every turn, even though I had on a private company's lanyard. Most inquiries had nothing to do with the surveys but were related to gate numbers, departure times, and so forth. We were contractors and had nothing directly to do with the bus station's day-to-day operations. However, I did my best to answer any questions or problems that I faced, even though I wasn't obligated to.

I happened to be standing nearby a terminal when I was on break. It was nearing noon when a Haitian passenger approached me. He asked me if the 11:00

a.m. bus had left. I did see it leave almost an hour beforehand and told him so. Couldn't he have figured it out at that time? He was probably too busy talking away on his cell phone, which he was still doing as we chatted. After I mentioned this seemingly shocking news to him, his demeanor changed instantly. He went from a normal facial appearance to a very angry one. He took his phone from his ear and came closer to me in a physically threatening manner. While doing so, he swore intermittently in English and French creole. I'm sure he was probably saying it to me, but maybe he was just speaking in general to blow off steam. I didn't say a word but was completely ready for him, no matter what he wished to do. He then just turned and walked away. Most likely, he went to the ticket counter and talked with them—hopefully in a nice way, but I doubt it. You can never be certain in any situation whether or not race plays a role. If I was Haitian, things might have gone a bit differently.

December 11, 2014

I had a great one-day job at working for a concierge company in Newton Upper Falls. The company was hired by a famous online travel agency as a benefit for their employees. I was with another temp, and we worked alongside several permanent workers. We had to wrap the employees' personal Christmas/holiday gifts. As I went along and wrapped the gifts, it just seemed a little impersonal to me. If the service was ever offered to me, I'd decline and happily do it myself—but no biggie. I can understand the hassle and time constraints that life can bring to people. It was one of the company's benefits. I overheard one employee say that it was her favorite benefit of all. She was probably just excited about the Christmas joy in the air. I can't imagine she preferred it over a matching 401k or the thrill of dental coverage and so forth. But all of the employees seemed to have appreciated our diligence in the fine art of wrapping. I suppose we could have made it more entertaining if we wrapped while rapping! Ready, now, one, two, three—Santa says wrap those gifts; don't you get the gist? Then again, maybe not. The whole experience was more enjoyable and Christmas-like due to the fact that it was snowing and because my contact's name was—you guessed it—Noelle.

Insecurity

May 8-12, 2015; May 18–June 12, 2015; June 16-26, 2015; July 28-29, 2015; August 4-5, 2015; August 18-20, 2015

I worked for a medical device contractor at many different hospitals on six separate occasions. The second time that I worked there brought some problems. Both my agency and my contractor's agency went through a lot of trouble to get me the correct ID badge that the hospital required. The first several days were fine, as security looked at my badge. It was different, however, on my way back from lunch one day. I walked by a security guard whom I had never seen before. The next thing I knew, he yelled, "Where are you going?" He then looked up at the camera and spoke into his lapel two-way radio, as a police officer in an emergency does. I had my badge on as usual, so I took it off and gave it to him to scrutinize. He said it wasn't the right badge. Instead I had to get a generic pink visitor's badge.

So let me get this straight. I had an official contractor's badge that was issued by the hospital. My name and photo were on it, along with my agency's name. But this was the wrong badge. Instead, the guard embarrassed me in front of many people, gave a generic pink visitor's badge with no identification whatsoever, and sneered at me. As I passed by him with my new excellent credentials, he again talked into his radio and explained all was safe now to whoever was listening on the other end. What a jerk. I knew of security guards who were sometimes policeman wannabes, but this was ridiculous.

A week passed, and I continued to wear my official pass with no problem. And then it happened again—but this time it was a female security guard who stopped me. As I put my tail between my legs and went to fetch the silly pink badge, guess who strolled over? The same jerk walked over to his female peer and told her that I was "caught" last week trying to do the same thing—which was what, following the hospital's rules? After that I decided to just get the silly pink pass on a daily basis and say to hell with my official badge. So I guess I was only a visitor and not a contractor to whoever cared about such matters.

Side Note:

PINK AGAIN?

We had some help from some permanent employees of the hospital. When certain medical devices were updated, there were different color stickers to signify that the update had been done. This was supposed to be a yearly task. This particular year was green. About a week passed, and it turned to pink somehow. As different random employees came to help us, they were never told that pink was the new green. No one seemed to know how this happened or even why. Some employees still used green, and some used pink, and of course the project was majorly screwed up. This had nothing to do with us contactors directly, as we had different tasks to do with the devices, so we just rolled our eyes. I noticed that they also used check marks on the stickers to signify yet another process was completed. The check marks were then changed at another juncture to check marks with lines drawn through them. Someone commented that the process must be changed due to the fact that the checkmarks with lines drawn through them looked like swastikas! They really did too.

Side Note:

IT'S A BIRD...IT'S A PLANE...

There was a small airport that was very close to the hospital. It looked like it was mostly for private jets. On some days the jets roared directly over the roof of the building every five to ten minutes. They were preparing for their landings. There was a large collection of pigeons around the various hospital structures as well, and sometimes when the noisy jets were overhead, I noticed that the pigeons were gliding from building to building with their outstretched wings. It appeared that the jet noise was coming directly from the pigeons as they were about to land! It was a funny scene that I witnessed time and again.

Militempy

I was just a kid in basic training in the military when I suffered a slight injury. While in the sick bay, I bunked with people with much more serious injuries and illnesses than I had. What we were offered was a surprise to me. Choice number one was to wait your time, have your injury heal, and join a new flight of recruits who were at the same level (let's say three weeks as an example) as you at the time of your injury. Choice number two was to simply go home permanently. I couldn't believe, after all we had signed up to do—the swearing-in ceremony and signing your life way (no turning back) and the money invested in each individual by the government—that we were just able to go home that easily if we chose.

For some reason, I just decided to go home. I wasn't having a particularly hard time with training or anything, and it wouldn't have been that long for me to rejoin a flight. But when the shocking option opened up to me, I just grabbed it. I guess I was just a young kid who knew that opportunities were everywhere (in the military or not), and so I made a choice.

I never felt guilty about leaving, and I respect to the fullest all of our people in uniform. If leaving would not have been an option, I would have been enlisted for years to come, which is what I had signed up to do. The decision was quick and without much consideration. It was only recently, after all these years had passed, that I even made the connection between my temporary role in the military and the life I've come to know as temporary in more ways than one. I guess that was an inadvertent start for my desire to always move on to the next gig.

Side note:

MY GREAT FRIEND SHAWN

I met a great guy there in the sick bay named Shawn, and we're still great friends to this day. He had a knee injury and decided to go home as well for his own reasons. On April 10–13, 2014, we made a visit to our home base after almost exactly twenty-five years. I left from Boston and he from Indianapolis. Though we were only there briefly back in the day, we did have our share of memories, good and bad. It was very strange to be back on the base. For some reason, we even got to walk freely with no restrictions—right up to where we got screamed at and worked out. We saw other new recruits being chewed out, and it was pretty funny. In some ways it was like no time whatsoever had passed by. I filmed some of it as an added memory. It was great seeing my buddy and reliving some of the good ol' times.

(Almost) On-the-Job Risks

JOMO FELL

was getting ready for work one morning when I happened to look out the window. What I witnessed was the single most hilarious chain of events that I ever have seen even to this day. We all have seen funny things multiple times in life, but rarely do we see many consecutive comical events. It was like a Vaudeville act or something. I'll try to explain the chain as well as I can.

An across-the-street Kenyan neighbor named Jomo was the star of this skit (unknowingly). I never told him, since I didn't think he'd appreciate it; we've both moved since then, so I'll never have the chance. I only wish I had it on video. It was a cool winter's morning. Jomo stepped out of the door of his three-family apartment. He took a few steps to reach the top of the stairs. He then paused before going down the stairs while looking up and around seemingly to say, "Good morning, world." He had a coffee mug in hand, and then he took his first step down toward infamy. He fell right on his back and slid down the entire flight of stairs while his mug flew in the air. He did fall safely, though. It could have been much worse if he had fallen head over heels or in another horrible position, but he lucked out. There had been freezing rain the night before, but I guess he thought it was warmer than that outside, so he wasn't at all careful.

He got up, turned to his right side, and looked back up the stairs, probably wondering what the hell had happened. His car was parked right there, and of course the windows were all frozen too. He opened the trunk to get a water jug so he could pour water on the icy windows to defrost them. As he tried to pour the water on from the jug, nothing came out— because it was obviously frozen too (as if cold water would have worked anyway). He looked perplexed as he peered into the jug. He then walked *very* carefully up the stairs while retrieving his mug and came back out a few minutes later with a bucket of steaming water. If he had fallen down with that, there's no telling what the outcome could have been. Instead, he made it down safely and first poured the hot water onto the back window. He poured it too strongly, though, so the water bounced off the window and right onto his crotch area and legs! He jumped slightly but continued on to the other windows, so I guess no damage was done. There could have been devastating results to the private area, so most likely the water was only lukewarm, even though it was steaming. He finally left for work, and I wondered if anything else ever happened that morning or day to him. To this day I remember exactly how the fall sounded even through the closed window. Now, was that one of the greatest starts in the history of the morning? Thanks for the memories, Jomo.

NEWS THAT DIDN'T MAKE THE PAPER

Some years ago I was on my way to an assignment in the morning. I was on a train, and I was about to exit at a certain doorway. There happened to be one guy in front of me and no one else around us at this particular exit as we approached the stop. The guy mumbled something without turning around. Before what he said could register in my brain, he raised his voice slightly and presumably repeated himself while still facing forward. He said, "Take the paper off me, or I'll kill you." The first time he definitely didn't say the "I'll kill you" part, as that would've been a really obvious phrase that would quickly register in anyone's brain.

We were both holding the same pole on the train. I had a newspaper folded in half, pretty small and lightweight, that chanced to be brushing lightly on his hand. I moved it away quickly, but I didn't say anything. His comments could have been racially motivated since he was black and I'm white, but you never really know. I'm very courteous usually, but this time didn't warrant an apology. I was angered, which is extremely rare. But if you're threatening my life, you'll experience an instant demeanor change in me. The funny thing was, I was a lot bigger and more muscular than him. What made him think he could kill me? If he was an assassin, how he would know I wasn't too? If he was a second-degree black belt, couldn't I have been a fourth? He wasn't armed; he had only a tight T-shirt and shorts on. Most guys would have said something back, and there would have been a skirmish—especially since I had the huge advantage of being directly behind him. I'm non-confrontational, though, and it was probably a good thing for him. The doors opened, we went our separate ways, and that was the end of that. Life goes on.

JUST IN TIME

In September 2014, I was again riding the train to a job when this time something funny and potentially dangerous happened. A really large man, both tall and heavy, was nearing his train stop. Although it was a little unusual to bring a bike on the train, he did have one with him that was pretty large. As the train operator braked for the stop, the man stood up and grabbed a pole to hold on to while simultaneously trying to secure his bike so it wouldn't fly into someone. He was able to do it. But as the train came to a complete stop, with all of the added pressure and inertia, the guy couldn't manage both the bike and his weight any longer. He fell down to one knee in a twisted-pretzel sort of way, with his head down as if he were praying to his bike, which he still held onto somehow. What he didn't hold onto was a banana peel, which he dropped right in front of the doors that were just about to open to masses of unwitting people. He managed to pick it up just in time, but as a result he almost lost his balance completely. That would have been very painful for him and others he might have crashed into. This whole situation was like a SNL skit or something.

MR. U

On December 9, 2014, I was on the way home from a job and saw something funny on the train. A guy got up from his seat, as his stop was coming. As he was getting up, he had a "lift-off" moment. His umbrella, while still on the seat, completely opened up and pushed up directly on his rear end while he was already in the motion of standing up. He turned around with a bewildered look on his face. Of course he had forgotten his umbrella. I guess Mr. Umbrella was offended, since he was abandoned after all. The guy must have thought he was being pushed by somebody or something. It was such an odd thing to see, and I've never witnessed anything like it. My best guess is that he must have secured it when he sat down initially and then sat directly on the open/close button or latch. I laughed with him as he realized what happened. I said, "He's mad that you forgot him." He again laughed, grabbed his buddy, and left the train. I wonder if he'll share his story with anyone. If not, I've got it covered.

ARE YOU SURE YOU WANT IT?

In June 2015, I was coming home from work on a commuter train. It was very hot out, so I decided to stand and hold on to the pole. I didn't want to get stuck to the seat. The conductor came by and gave me my seat-check ticket, as I had a weekly pass. I held it for many stops while holding the pole with my sweaty hand. When it came time for him to retrieve the ticket, he had to peel it off of my hand. We both smiled—a silly yet sticky situation.

often discussed temp jobs with my grandfather Boompa, may he rest in peace. He called it job shopping, which I guess is the older term. Nowadays, we know it as temporary, temp-hire, contract staffing, and so on. Some of his most interesting and well-paying jobs came from his job-shopping techniques. He would always enjoy hearing about my current job adventure. He never questioned or pressured me to seek out a permanent full-time job. We definitely bonded on the subject, which might surprise a lot of people. During one visit, I told him an assignment had just ended for me, and I was going on vacation to Denmark right away. He thought it was the funniest thing. I had lost my job and was off to Europe? He supported my decision 100 percent! He knew I'd be back shortly and off to the next job (shop).

Don't I Know You?

Several Companies and Dates

On occasion I'd bump into my previous permanent coworkers going to work while I was on my way to different temp assignments. My feelings about seeing them varied depending on how long I worked at their particular company—and also how well I knew them. I would recall some of the times we had, good or bad. In a weird way, it was like I was cheating on them. Certain awkward conversations during some of these reunions led me to believe that they were thinking perhaps their company wasn't good enough for me, so I moved on to greener pastures. For this reason I would sometimes avoid them by going onto a different train car. Alas, people often jump to conclusions.

No Companies or Dates, and Some Companies and Dates

'I've had my share of just missing some temp jobs. I know few details, since most of the time I just missed a call and never found out what the job even was. Someone else was chosen. Often the jobs were time sensitive, and the clients hadn't given any notice. It was only one time that I actually went to the job and still missed it. When I got to the Boston high rise, the front-desk security called my contact, who was angry that the other temp for the day was a no-show. She yelled at me on the security guard's phone. I had no idea another temp was even supposed to be there. As a result, I was sent home before I was allowed to even meet my contact and have a chance to make things right. My agency apologized and also paid me for several hours. Darn it, I was so close to being able to save face for my company. I was almost a walking coffee cup for donut-shop promo. I was almost a Pilgrim or possibly even a turkey for a software company during a Thanksgiving promo. And finally, I was almost a shirtless supermodel. OK, I'm exaggerating a little. There was a one-day job at a hospital where a group of doctors was going to be present. I was to take my shirt off and put on electrodes, among other things, and be studied for the day. It would have been a very interesting and well-paying gig. I wonder what the objective was. Oh well, you can't win them all.

In other cases, I'd just barely get the job. Sometimes clients don't realize they need someone until the last minute. Other times one of their employees—permanent or temporary—has called in sick. And still other times, we never learn the reasons for their immediate need. Many times I'd be at home relaxing or just reading a book when suddenly my agency would call and ask if I could be at a given assignment within the hour. This would happen both day and night. I felt like Batman seeing the bat signal; I needed to act immediately. I had to turn them down sometimes, but only if I was out of town or had an appointment. Otherwise, I loved the urgency, unexpectedness, and excitement of it all. Where was I going to be, and what kind of job would I be doing within this hour? A lot of thoughts run through your head to be sure. I always looked forward to the spontaneity, even though last-minute calls were pretty rare.

October 9, 2014

This situation occurred during the writing of this chapter. At around 8:30 a.m., a call came in from an unfamiliar phone number that had popped up on my cell. The caller was a representative from my agency who was out in the field on his personal phone. He asked if I was available to come to a job ASAP. It happened to be with a large, well-known razor company, so I had the chance to work for yet another major company which was a good opportunity that I didn't want to miss. I gleefully told him I'd be there within the hour. Just as I was getting ready to leave, he called again. He asked me if I'd completed the prequalifying screening tests for drugs required for the job. What the heck? I knew nothing of the job, and he had just called me out of the blue. How was I supposed to know much less complete any test? (That's what I wanted to say.) He then asked me to call our office to sort out some details. I did so only to find out that he'd called the wrong Thomas in the first place. My agency gave him the wrong number but the right name. On to the next job…

Hollywood Was in Town Temporarily

Known and Unknown Companies and Dates

BITTERSWEET

I worked at the registration table for a conference on multiple sclerosis held at the JFK library in Boston. Actress Teri Garr has the condition and was the main speaker for the day. Most of the attendees of course also had MS. There were many people with wheelchairs or canes and others who walked with the help of leaning against another's shoulders or arms. I was concerned that once the actress arrived, there might be an injury or something with all of the excitement. I felt bad when she came, as she had such a bad limp and used a cane to help her walk the best she could. I thought about the movies that I had seen her in and how healthy and vibrant she was. It was great that she was here to help and support people with the same ailment. Before she spoke at the event, she sat at a table to sign autographs and talk with the attendees and fans. As I expected, there was a problem when the people crowded her. I helped out on some near misses, but thankfully no one fell or got inured at all. There were smiles abound, and a good, positive MS conference followed, with lots of cheering and positive reinforcement to be seen and heard. I'm glad we're closer to a cure today than we were all those years ago.

TOM WORKING JUST OUTSIDE THE DOOR FROM TOM

In the fall of 2009, I was working at a job in a small building in Charlestown. It happened to be one of the sites where Knight and Day starring Tom Cruise was being filmed. It was an exciting several days for us workers to see a film shoot and maybe catch a glimpse of Tom Terrific. We didn't have any advanced notice of any building restrictions whatsoever when I worked on one Saturday. When I arrived, the large parking lot was completely full of the Hollywood moviemakers and everything that comes with them. There were trailers full of stunt dummies and all sorts of different types of stunt cars. There were lights and cameras but no action yet. People darted here and there, doing all sorts of assignments. I had to walk through the parking lot to get to my building to work. A security guard met me at the gate. I told him that I worked in the building. He wouldn't let me by, and I wasn't happy about it, especially since I didn't get any notice about the day's activities. I decided to force my way by; he didn't say a word. I visually took in as much as I could see, figuring I'd never see anything else like it again. At the end of my workday, I again walked through the parking lot as they were also wrapping up their day. Those stunt dummies looked really dumb up close; people were folding them up for the next location.

It turned out that while we worked inside all day, Tom filmed a scene right outside our lunchroom window. I did not see it but did watch it a few days later on a coworker's cell phone. It seemed so fake to see something filmed behind the scenes. Presumably, the fact that Tom was such a big star would explain the reason why an SUV pulled up right to the scene. He got out and did his scene and was quickly escorted back to the SUV and driven on his way. I'm only guessing that other actors actually mingle with the film crews, but I could be totally wrong. Maybe this is always how it works. Who knows? The street in front of the building was blocked off where the filming took place. Right behind the street is part of an old highway that still stands today. That's where they filmed some vehicles flipping over onto their tops for some great crash scenes. Tom could have joined us for lunch, but no one invited him. I heard there were a lot of screams and shrieks when the women filmed him outside the window. Shame on them for not inviting him.

EYES REALLY ARE MIRRORS TO THE SOUL

I took another lunch break from a temp job to meet Frank Abagnale. He was played by Leo DiCaprio in the movie Catch Me If You Can. He is a reformed con artist who was in Boston as part of a national tour for an office superstore. He was peddling a shredding machine that shredded papers not just vertically but horizontally as well. If you shred only vertically as he explained, he could tape the small pieces back together and read your personal papers. He spontaneously signed a few autographs for people who were his fans. For fun, I approached him and pretended that I never heard of him. We briefly touched on the subject of his life. I asked questions about the product and he gave me his business card in case I had any more questions. The whole time, his eyes were rapidly shifting left to right while directly looking into my eyes. As a former con man he needed to be a quick study among other things. One probably never loses that skill. He knew that I knew of him through the cross examination.

GREAT COMEDIC TIMING

During lunch one day, while on a temporary job, I decided to see a food workshop. Celebrity chef Ming Tsai was holding it in a Boston department store. The samples were delicious, thanks. Billy Costa was the actual host. He has a local Boston area TV show that has him visit interesting food destinations/restaurants. I guess the two of them must have known each other for years. I base this on the hilarious banter they had with each other. I've never even seen two comedians who came close to their comedic connection. What a pleasant unexpected surprise. The joy, however, morphed into super awkwardness for me. Ming had a book signing afterwards which I was interested in. People almost always rush at a celebrity for anything, especially a book signing. I decided that I'd wait a few minutes for the crowd to die down and then get my book signed. Well, it didn't work out that smoothly. After the last few got their book signed, he got distracted while talking to several people. It was probably his manager or assistant and store management too. Anyway, I did not want to interrupt him so I patiently waited. He walked away from his table and headed my way. He didn't know that I was seeking him out. There was a narrow corridor between two tables and as we met up he turned his body away while walking and talking to someone that was nearby. I sort of naturally did the same thing and turned away and as a result we completely rubbed butts. I'm talking two cheeks squished on two cheeks people. I decided that introduction was better than an autograph and departed as quickly as possible.

Please feel free to read my temp blog or share stories of your own temp job adventures at thomasthetempjobking@squarespace.com

I'm also for hire so please feel free to inquire.